CHRISTMAS IN BETHLEHEM

CHRISTMAS IN BETHLEHEM

AND HOLY WEEK AT MOUNT ATHOS

CHRISTOPHER RAND

NEW YORK · OXFORD UNIVERSITY PRESS · 1963

TO MY FAMILY

ACKNOWLEDGMENTS

This whole work was undertaken by *The New Yorker* and me together, and without *The New Yorker* it could not have been done.

I have also been helped by innumerable friends in Palestine, Greece, and the United States. I cannot list them all, but they know what they did for me, and I trust they know how thankful I am.

CONTENTS

PART ONE

CHRISTMAS IN BETHLEHEM

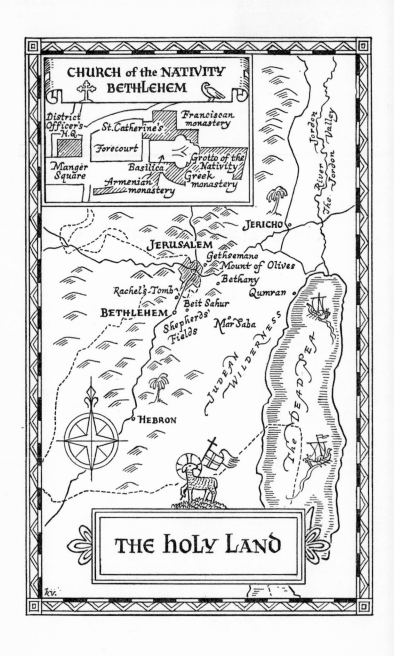

CHURCH of the NATIVITY
BETHLEHEM

District Officer's H.Q.

St. Catherine's

Franciscan monastery

Forecourt

Manger Square

Basilica

Armenian monastery

Grotto of the Nativity

Greek monastery

JERICHO

River Jordan

The Jordan Valley

JERUSALEM

Gethsemane

Mount of Olives

Bethany

Rachel's Tomb

Qumran

Beit Sahur

BETHLEHEM

Shepherds' Fields

Mar Saba

JUDEAN WILDERNESS

THE DEAD SEA

HEBRON

THE HOLY LAND

kv.

The Latin Christmas

On a recent christmas eve I went to Bethlehem in the
procession of His Beatitude Alberto Gori, the Roman
Catholic, or "Latin," Patriarch of Jerusalem. The Catholic
services at Bethlehem didn't start till late that afternoon,
but His Beatitude, by ancient custom, went there at midday — leaving from his Patriarchate in Jerusalem — and
I was on hand to follow him.

The Patriarchate is a large, palatial, primitive building,
medieval in aspect, and made of buff limestone like nearly
all Jerusalem. It stands just inside the Old City's crenellated wall, beyond which — and visible through an em-
brasure — lies a no-man's-land and then, in the distance,
Jerusalem's newer, Israeli sector. That new part has wide
streets and whizzing traffic, but this Old City around the
Patriarchate has changed but little since the Crusaders
ruled it, and partly rebuilt it, in the twelfth century.
Through most of it one can move only on narrow, twisting
alleys — which often change into stairways — but there are
two motorable streets as well, paved and leveled in modern
times, which pass out by two of the seven old gates. One of

3

them goes from the Latin Patriarchate itself, and so His Beatitude was making the whole trip to Bethlehem by car.

His start had been prepared before I got there. Two steps — of limestone, inevitably — led down from the Patriarchal courtyard to the street, and on each of them two little wooden ramps had been placed, for the car's left and right wheels. The car itself — it was a black seven-passenger Chrysler sedan — was waiting in the courtyard, an enclosure with wide stairs descending from the Patriarchal residence and offices. From one of the car's front fenders rose a small flag, yellow and white, bearing the double-barred cross of Lorraine, and the flag's metal standard was crowned by a similar cross — it is an emblem used especially, I have since learned, by patriarchs, archbishops, and other primates of the Church.

While I was looking at these things, ten Jordanian policemen drove up to the Patriarchate in two khaki Land-Rovers, or British jeeps. They parked in the street, got out, and stood around — they were dressed in their regulation winter uniform, which is of rough, thick khaki, with khaki helmets topped by spikes. They were friendly — two of them spoke good English — and they began telling me about the arrangements for the procession. It would contain only five cars at first, they said. Besides the black Chrysler and the two Land-Rovers, there was a gray De Soto waiting nearby, to carry secondary priests and prelates, and finally there was a little Fiat sedan, with a huge driver, that was my own conveyance. I had hired it through my hotel and was lucky to have it — hordes of Christmas tourists, now gathered in Jerusalem, had engaged all the available taxis for sightseeing in the daytime and convergence on Bethlehem later on.

I waited in the street, amid yellow limestone walls that

glowed in the sun. A few little Arab boys were around —
they always are, in street scenes of the Old City. A little
donkey with a huge load on his back walked by. Then suddenly there was a pealing of bells; priests appeared; people
got into cars; and without quite knowing how it happened
we were off. We drove for some time through Jerusalem,
with limestone masonry on either hand. Then we went
out through a gate and were in the country. The road was
tortuous after it left the city. It doubled back, swooped
down a hill, went by the Garden of Gethsemane, then
straightened to the southward, Bethlehem's direction.

We did all this at a good speed. In our van was a Land-
Rover of policemen, then came His Beatitude's Chrysler,
then the other Land-Rover, then the De Soto full of lesser
priests, and then our Fiat. Now and then — as we snaked
around curves — I got glimpses of His Beatitude. He was
a thickset man with a white beard. He wore dark robes and
a wide-brimmed, flat clerical hat, with a green pompon
on it. At his right, in the back seat, there sat another prelate, somewhat taller, with a crimson biretta, and in the
front seat were an ordinary priest, at the wheel, and a
kawass, or Arab sergeant-at-arms, wearing a fez and a brocaded livery. The second Patriarchal car, the De Soto, held
an Arab driver, one monsignor with a black biretta, two
canons with wide flat hats and white beards like His Beatitude, and one other priest whom I did not identify. Later
I learned that the man riding with the Patriarch, in the
crimson biretta, was Monsignor Joseph Ryan of Albany,
a member of the Pontifical Mission for Palestine refugees
in Beirut.

The day was lovely, with a pure blue sky, and we sped
on freely in the open. The countryside looked dry, and in
fact I had heard many complaints in Jerusalem of drought.

The day before, a Russian nun, in a convent on the Mount
of Olives, had told me how her order had closed its pri-
mary school in nearby Bethany for lack of water. "We
can't get water for the girls to drink or wash with," she
had said, "and we can't go on that way. The whole situation here is terrible. Sheep are being sold for a third of
their normal price, because there is no grass. It is a catas-
trophe."

But for processions it wasn't catastrophic, I felt, as we
bounded on in the sun. The rainy season should have begun by now, and the fields should have been tinged with
green. But instead the ground was tawny — dry and dusty,
almost white. Here and there it had pale limestone out-
crops, and the stone and ground were so alike in tone as
to be unearthly. We passed a flock of sheep, lying on a
hillside, and they could hardly be distinguished from their
background. But there were other colors too: the black
of goats, the dark green of cypresses, the greenish gray of
olives. In some spots the ground had just been plowed,
and it was darker there. But on the whole it was colored
like the stone, and peppered with it also—rocky everywhere. The houses were of limestone, too, and they stood
out from the background not in color but in form. They
were square and sharp, like cubical stone boxes.

The land was hilly, and the road went up and down
the slopes in zigzags. It was a new, emergency road, built
in the past decade, because the old one to Bethlehem from
Jerusalem is mainly in Israeli hands now. The new road
is twice as long as the old, I have been told, because of the
hills and switchbacks. We hurried along it. Often the head
of our procession would pass some other cars, and our Fiat
would be stuck behind them — struggling to stay in the
parade — around the curves. I spoke no Arabic, and my

driver little English, so as a rule he just sat there, hugely and silently, and drove, while I surveyed the scene.

After twenty minutes, perhaps, of speedy travel, we reached the junction where the old road comes in, from across the Israeli border. We stopped there for a moment and were greeted by a few men wearing the fez or *tarboosh* — the red Middle Eastern hat, that is, with the black tassel. But we didn't linger. We hurried on again, and in five more minutes we came to a famous landmark, the tomb of Rachel, wife of the patriarch Jacob, where a goodly crowd was waiting. Mostly they were men in Arab headgear — *tarbooshes* or *kafiyahs*, the flowing scarves worn in the desert. Some were Moslem notables, I gathered later, and others Arab Christians; and they came from Bethlehem and nearby villages. They had turned out to meet us, and, when our cars had stopped, His Beatitude descended from the Chrysler, and the crowd filed by to kiss his hand.

Off to one side were eight or ten men on horses — "They are knights," an Arab told me later, in uncertain English, but actually they were troopers of the Jordan police. They wore uniforms much like our escort's, but with boots and breeches. They had good Arab horses, and they sat them well, and each man held a lance with pennant. Their presence was one sign, of many, that we had become a real parade; and presently, the hand-kissing over, we formed up to journey on. There were many new cars in our procession now, and it moved but slowly, for the horsemen rode beside the Patriarch and set the pace; they jogged with liveliness, but not much forward speed.

We were nearing Bethlehem — we had already been glimpsing it from the road. It hadn't stood out much in the distance — a tawny settlement on a tawny hill. Rachel's Tomb, a small domed structure in off-white, could be

called an outpost of it. After that the buildings, always
of stone masonry, grew thicker, and the crowds grew
thicker too. They stood on the hillsides and watched us,
and they clapped their hands and crossed themselves as
the Patriarch went by.

Soon we got into real streets — narrow, with taller
houses flanking them — and people were standing in the
doorways. We heard bells ringing here and there. We
passed a convent, where nuns were standing. We drove
under a stone arch. Children were running beside us now,
and the street was lined with people. It twisted up a hill
and doubled back confusingly, and it was so narrow that
the horsemen could no longer ride beside the Chrysler.
We were halted sometimes, too, in the congestion — once
before a shop where a radio was blaring out gay music.

Yet bit by bit we went along, and finally we burst into
an open space, a square. It was thronged with people, gay
with decorations, and resonant with bells and other music.
The Fiat stopped, and I got out, and a band was playing
Adeste Fideles. Through the crowded heads I glimpsed a
Franciscan monk, singing with gusto and leading others
in song. Then I saw His Beatitude again, now wearing a
crimson biretta and an ermine stole. He was moving
through the crowd, behind a file of priests in colored vestments. He moved off the scene that way and left it to the
multitude.

The space in which I found myself was called, and
plainly labeled, Manger Square. It was oblong, flanked on
its greater sides by buildings, with some open lots. One
end led back to the narrow streets by which we had come,
and the other opened up still wider, to a plaza beyond
which rose a massive, medieval complex of buildings —

the Church of the Nativity, this was, with some flanking monasteries. It had been the goal of our procession, and it is, indeed, the goal of much Christian endeavor throughout the world, for it stands on the site where Christ, supposedly, was born.

That was the direction in which the Patriarch had gone, but I did not follow there myself. According to plan, His Beatitude would retire for a few hours in a Franciscan monastery that adjoined the church's northern side. Meanwhile, I thought, I would spend the afternoon exploring Bethlehem and taking in some other festivities — most notably a carol-singing fest, arranged by the Y.M.C.A., in the nearby Shepherds' Fields. Then I would return for the Catholic ceremonies in the evening.

The crowd thinned out in Manger Square. The place's name is thought offensive by some Christians, and a rather tinny style of publicity — of mercenary huckstering — does afflict the holy town. Near the church and Manger Square one finds many shops and peddlers, aggressively selling knickknacks and religious items. Some of the latter, like rosaries and crucifixes, are of lovely native olivewood, but the town's great specialty is mother-of-pearl mosaics. These are made in small workshops round about, where the pearl is cut in tiny pieces and stuck together again, to form religious scenes. The most ambitious subject, as a rule, is the Last Supper, good specimens of which may take months of work to finish. Their value as art is questionable, and some visitors deplore the trade in them. Yet at least that trade is time-honored, for it was founded by the Crusaders centuries ago, when they ruled Bethlehem, as a way of feeding the hungry.

The Crusaders left other traces in the town, too, aside from its architecture, which has much in common with

medieval Europe's. The women of Bethlehem wear, traditionally, a headdress — like a tablecloth draped on a
cone — such as one often sees in portraits of medieval
women. This is said, perhaps erroneously, to be a Crusader legacy. Then there are many blond heads and blue
eyes in Bethlehem, and these are often laid, genetically,
to the Crusaders' sojourn. "They were here for a hundred
years," an Arab guide once told me, "and human nature,
after all, is human nature." And he shrugged his shoulders.

Be that as it may, Bethlehem is a relatively Christian
town — it has a high proportion, that is, of Christian Arabs
compared with Moslem ones. This fact is probably *not*
the Crusaders' work, primarily, for the Bethlehem Christians belong more to the Eastern churches than the Roman
Catholic; yet anyway the whole town seemed to have come
out now, to greet the Roman Patriarch.* Many people must
have traveled in from elsewhere, too — from Jerusalem
and the villages. The place was thronged like a county
fair. Then with the Patriarch's disappearance, as I have
said, the crowd began to drift away, going off to homes, tea-
shops, and other crannies.

I had brought some sandwiches and beer with me; and
a soldier of the Arab Legion — the Jordanian army — let
me take it into the cab of a Legion truck that was standing
there (for I had let the Fiat go). I sat in the truck for some
time, nibbling and sipping, and presently a little black
sedan, with a poster on it advertising coffee, drove up and
parked nearby. It was a commercial stunt, apparently, for
a young man in a *tarboosh* got out, holding a small drum
in his hand, and began to amuse the crowd. He sat on the

---

* Who is locally known, however, as the Latin Patriarch, "Latin" being the
standard Holy Land term for the Church that uses Latin in its services
and is called Roman or Catholic or both by us Westerners.

radiator and recited what seemed to be patter songs, accompanying them with rhythms on the drum. He soon showed himself to be a gifted mountebank — a real clown, giving a real county-fair performance — and he gathered the fragments of the crowd and held them tight. When I finished my lunch and left the truck he was burlesquing a belly-dancer, it seemed; and a hundred people were round him all attention.

I walked out of Manger Square to the east and slightly north, taking the Church of the Nativity on my right — I didn't study it then, but was just vaguely conscious of it, as a big array of masonry. When I passed it, Jerusalem was to my left — five miles distant and out of sight beyond the landscape. The Dead Sea, on the other hand, was right ahead of me, and visible; at least one edge of it was — a sliver of blue, low down beyond the tawny hills. It was fifteen miles away. Just short of it lay the Judean Wilderness, a semi-desert zone where nomads range; and short of that, again, lay more settled — better-watered — country. In some part of this, supposedly, the shepherds saw the angel on the night when Christ was born. That was the country toward which I was headed now, and it lay below me, down a hill.

The road was narrow, squeezed between buildings and a wall, and I traveled downward on the asphalt pavement. Then it all widened out, and I could walk on the ground alongside — though this was hard, too, and dusty. I passed a flock of sheep beneath some trees. They had fat tails, long Roman noses, brown faces, and beige wool. I was out of Bethlehem now, and almost down the hill, but immediately I came to another village, called Beit Sahur. I went on through this. Two or three times I came to a fork or crossing, where I didn't know the way, but when I paused there, wondering, people would come up — even little children — to direct me. We didn't really have to speak — they were very friendly, and they seemed to know my destination.

I got out of Beit Sahur and began finding signposts for the Shepherds' Fields, in English; but three "Shepherds' Fields" were noted, then and later — those of the Y.M.C.A., of the Greek Orthodox Church, and of the Roman Catholic. I held for the Y.M.C.A. site that afternoon, but later I came back and saw the others. The Greek site is the nearest one to Bethlehem — it is off to the right, just after Beit Sahur. All that remains there is the crypt of a former church, with rough stone steps going down to its wooden door. Above ground there is nothing but scanty ruins, with pasture and olive trees around them. The Shepherds' Fields of the Catholics come next — they are off to the left and well out in the country. That site, too, has ruins on it, and it also has a new domed chapel, Byzantine in style, with murals in it of the shepherds' story. Then finally the Y.M.C.A. has *its* Fields, still farther out.

Later I read about these various Shepherds' Fields, and their differing claims to authenticity. The Greek site has the oldest history — the ruins there are supposed, by archeologists, to be from a fourth-century church. The Catholic ruins are old, too, yet they are thought to come not from a church but from a monastery or farm. Then as for the Protestant — Y.M.C.A. — site, it has no old remains at all, but is merely a piece of land, bought a few years ago, in the general region where the shepherds might, conceivably, have seen their vision. In the eyes of some observers, at least, the Greek Fields have the best claim to authenticity, because they were regarded in early Christian

times as the true site; they have the longest tradition behind them, that is — "tradition" being a useful concept,
popular in the Holy Land, for assigning relative value to
sites, or stories, for which no real historical evidence exists.
No one knows where, in that country east of Bethlehem,
the shepherds really saw the angel (if they did); but "tradition," on the whole, favors the Greek site. No one, for
that matter, knows that the site *was* east of Bethlehem —
it might, so far as true records go, have been in any other
direction — but "tradition" says it was east; and the Christian world, in its different ways, has gone along with this.*

The region of the Fields made a likely scene, at least, I

* Indeed it is only tradition — to anticipate a bit — that places Christ's
birth on the site where the Church of the Nativity now stands — there is
no record, in the Bible or elsewhere, that can be used to prove the spot.
The Bible does place the birth in Bethlehem as a whole — it is so recorded
in the Gospels of Saint Matthew and Saint Luke — but even these records
are only traditional in that they were written long after the event, by
people without close knowledge of it. The Bethlehem Nativity is, in fact,
questioned by some scholars. Luke's and Matthew's accounts are different,
these scholars point out — Luke mentions only the shepherds, Matthew
only the wise men; Luke has the Nativity taking place in a stable, Matthew
has Joseph and Mary living in a house then; Luke has them in Bethlehem
as transients, for tax purposes, while Matthew seems to have them in fixed
abode there, and leaving, later, only through fear of Herod. Then elsewhere the Gospels hint that Christ's life may have begun not in Bethlehem
but in Galilee, where he grew up. In view of these things some scholars —
a minority, be it said — suspect that the Nativity story was placed in Bethlehem wishfully, by early Christian apologists, so as to match Old Testament prophecies (notably that of Micah: "But thou Bethlehem Ephrathah,
though thou be little among the thousands of Judah, yet out of thee shall
he come forth unto me that is to be ruler in Israel"). It is known that the
Jewish people were feverishly expecting a Messiah in Christ's time, and
he was supposed to come from the house of David, which was identified
with Bethlehem. In some Jewish minds the validity of Christ's calling may
have hung on questions like this; and Christians may have been tempted,
in the controversies of the day, to bend their facts accordingly. Or so it
has been argued.

thought as I journeyed on. I was a mile or two from Bethlehem by now — an easy distance for the shepherds to have
traveled for their adoration. And the landscape, too, seemed
shepherdly, though much of it today was cultivated. It was
about three o'clock in the afternoon now, and the sun was
still warm. Ever since Beit Sahur the road had been of
dirt — hard and dusty, inescapably. Now it was running
between jagged stone walls, with bare brown fields beyond
them. Sometimes I passed little stone houses, and orchards
of bare, dry-looking fig and almond trees. I passed women
in long dresses, and their skirts made a rhythmic, billow-
ing sound as they strode by. The terrain was soft and rolling, and almost wholly bare except for the trees, the stone
walls, and the houses. It looked like certain landscapes in
Italian paintings.

In time I saw a sign, off to the road's left, saying "FIELD
OF THE SHEPHERDS, PROPERTY JERUSALEM YMCA." I went a
little farther, turned in by a gate — it had stone posts with
glass stars, electrically illuminable, on them — and found
myself looking at a stone building, new and substantial, and
reminiscent of those on some American parkways. It was
surrounded by evergreens, apparently planted some years
ago, which screened most of the nearby landscape from
view. But the vista back to Bethlehem was clear, and what
I saw there was the outline of a nice sharp stone-house
town, with towers and some trees, on a ridgeline three
miles distant.

An Arab servant — perhaps a caretaker — stood outside
the Y.M.C.A. building, and he told me that the singing itself would be at a spot nearby, toward which he pointed.
Other visitors were arriving, too, though the festivities
were not due for half an hour. Most of them were tourists,
from America or West Europe, and most were dressed,

quite sensibly, as if for an autumn football game. Many carried cameras. Some were going into the stone building, where tea, coffee, and snacks could be bought. I went inside it, too, and had a look; then I came out again and went off in the direction that the caretaker had shown me.

A wide path ran that way, through the pine trees, and in a few minutes it came out on the other side of them, on a spot that overlooked a valley. There was a sizable enclosure there, bounded by a high fence, and in this I found some turfy ground with, in the middle of it, a shallow limestone pit leading to a limestone grotto. The enclosure could, and later did, accommodate a couple of thousand people easily. In the pit stood a harmonium; and a choir of some fifteen singers, mainly women, was gathered near it. A few visitors had come into the enclosure, too. Some were Arab Christians — who tend to be distinguishable, by their more Western dress, from Arab Moslems. Others were Western military men, from the various UN truce missions in that region — these wore khaki, with sky-blue UN berets. Then finally the bulk of the gathering — which grew steadily from then on — was made up of tourists like the ones I have mentioned. (I call them tourists, and not pilgrims, because I think their motives for coming to the scene were largely touristic — a matter of interest in strange places — rather than devotional. Few of them seemed to be doing anything like a penance, or expecting a mystical experience.)

The visitors drifted into the enclosure, but there was still some time left, so I drifted out. A high stone wall ran by the place on its downhill side, and then the ground sloped away below it, to a bare brown valley. Some Arab boys were playing outside the cyclone fence, and I walked past them and continued east, inside the wall. A round white moon had risen above the horizon. The sky was blue still, but darkening, and the hills across the valley looked like maple sugar. I leaned against the wall and watched three camels coming toward me, on a road at the valley's end. They had bulky loads, perhaps of brush for fuel, and three men were driving them.

I grew aware of people on the wall's other side — a poor family, they turned out to be, living in a cave there. They had some rabbits grazing on the turf, and a stone cooking-place in the open. Soon a little girl, perhaps five years old, appeared from their cave and asked for *baksheesh.* Her face was pretty, with eyes ringed by dark cosmetic in the Arab style. Then a boy, still smaller, came and asked for *baksheesh,* too. Then other members of the family came, and I dealt out some coins. There were lots of rabbits there, and soon an old man showed up, wearing a *kafiyah,* and began calling them to put them away for the night. "Wik wik, wik," he called, "wik, wik, wik;" and he half led, half drove the rabbits to a hole.

I went back to the enclosure, for the carols had begun. The crowd sang *The First Nowell.* The place seemed very quiet after they had finished, and then they began singing *O Come, All Ye Faithful.* I felt isolated, amid the singers, from the landscape, and so I left the enclosure once again. A stream of people was still entering as I went out. "We have two thousand here already," a Y.M.C.A. official told me at the gate, "and more are coming all the time."

I climbed over the big stone wall and went down the hill to a smaller one, a few dozen yards away; and I got up on this to recline and take in the scene. The sky was still darker now, and the moon was gleaming with a fuzzy ring around it. Crows were flying home, and the brown hills glowed in the dusk.

The people in the enclosure sang *Hark, the Herald Angels Sing*. They were tightly massed inside the fence, while outside it the Arab boys were moving freely, engaged in horseplay. Some of them played follow-the-leader, jumping off the stone wall, which was as high as their heads, and landing on some rocky ground below, but apparently doing it successfully. *Hark, the Herald Angels Sing* came to an end, and again the scene was quiet. I heard dogs barking far away, and on a distant ridge I made out a couple of settlements, with trees, that looked as if they might be villages or monasteries. I heard some strange bird-calls in the gloaming, too, and then the singers began on *Silent Night*.

Some of the Arab boys noticed me, came over, and began to joke with me in English. "The hyena will come!" one of them said in dramatic warning, and the others laughed (I found out later, incidentally, that hyenas do live in that countryside, or at least in the Judean Wilderness). The laughter died down, and the boys next asked for my address, so they could write to me some day. I scribbled it for them, and we discussed what a wonderful place New York was. Then they wrote down their addresses for me — they filled a page or two of my notebook with these, badly scrawled in the fading light. Then after that they turned their attention back to the carol-singers, and began to joke about them.

"They are fighting like bees!" one boy said.

"Do you mean like beasts?" I asked.

"No, like bees!" he answered, and the others laughed.

After that they began telling me that the wall was infested with snakes and insects, but I stood my ground — reclined on it, that is — courageously. Then one boy took out a flute and began playing an Arab tune, while the others sang and clapped their hands. We almost had a rival song-fest going, but by this time it was full moonlight, and presently the carols stopped, and I went back to the enclosure.

Many of the visitors were staying on, I found, for a light repast of Arab food. This was served in the grotto, which was a big domed chamber, like others I saw later in the Holy Land — they have all been formed, I suppose, by dissolution of the limestone. This one was lit up, now, by electric bulbs wired to a generator. The food was simply mutton served, in sandwich style, in flat round Arab bread. We filed by a trestle table to get our portions, dropping money in a plate as we did so, and most of the guests ate quickly, if at all, and left — they were returning, as a rule, to Jerusalem, for dinner and a rest, before driving back to Bethlehem in the evening.

I was planning to stay in the region, though, and I had been at the end of the line to start with, so I lingered almost alone in the cave while the crowd vanished and the lights dimmed down. Then suddenly eight Western ladies, well along in years, appeared and accosted me. They said that they were Christian Scientists, from Europe and America, and that they wished to hold a service in the cave and had permission to do so. But they wanted the electricity made stronger — it was too weak for reading now, they pointed out — and they asked if I could attend to this. I tried to convince them, but in vain, that I was an innocent bystander. Then I went away and found — and put them in touch with — the caretaker I had met earlier. And then I left.

The moon was not only fuzzy now, as I headed back on the road; it was dim and had a great wide ring around it.

But still it lit my way; and the visitors' cars, with their lights and noise, had passed off the scene already. I walked back through a dim gray countryside, as the shepherds might have done themselves. But the Bethlehem I saw was brighter than theirs could have been — it was lit by a galaxy of electric bulbs, till it seemed, in the distance, like some American town at night. Two lights, high up in the galaxy, shone with special brightness, and later I learned that these were electric crosses above the Church of the Nativity.

I walked on, passed through Beit Sahur, and started up to Bethlehem; and I found now that the hill was very steep. I labored up it, though, eventually. Then I passed the Church of the Nativity and went on to Manger Square. The place was brightly lit now, in the darkness, and it was once more crowded. As I approached it I saw knots of monks, nuns, children, soldiers, and policemen moving about at random, but dramatically — also lady tourists and Arabs with *kafiyahs*.

I passed them without lingering, though, for it was dinnertime and I was hungry — I had eaten little at the cave. In a store on a narrow street I found some wine, made by Salesian monks in Bethlehem's outskirts, and I bought a bottle and took it to a little food shop, where I ordered some sandwiches, again of Arab bread. Each loaf is thick but disc-shaped. The top and bottom don't stick together, and the Arabs cut the loaf in half — in semicircles — making two flat pouches, which they fill with various preparations. They filled some for me now, and I ate them and washed them down with the wine. The shop was a tiny cellar room, with massive stone vaulting overhead. A few more Arab schoolboys were in it, wanting — like those at the Fields — to display their English; and they, too, asked me for my address, and especially they gave me theirs and urged me to write.

I finished my meal and went back to Manger Square, which was getting more crowded all the time. The place was lined with food stalls selling things like cakes, shish kebab, and sandwiches — doing a raging business, they seemed to be, and often running out of supplies. There were many soldiers of the Arab Legion in the crowd — smart and tough looking — and there were little boys setting off fireworks, here and there, in the midst of things. Above the square hung colored lights, in swooping lines, and from one of its sides an irregular evergreen tree leaned out — like something in a Japanese garden, but much bigger — and it too was full of lights. Its trunk was wrapped with bunting, and in the middle of its branches was a big blue angel with the word GLORIA across its chest. A brass band of the Arab Legion was playing, then later some pipes and drums of the Legion, too — a reminder, these were, of the force's British training.

I watched the crowd awhile, then looked in on some shops. In one of them, called the Holy Land Stores, some American tourists were resting, the ladies seated on straight chairs. The shopkeeper was treating his guests to wine, and his business seemed to be good. Then I came back and watched the crowd some more. Beyond it rose the Church of the Nativity, with the two big crosses — plus an electric star — shining out in the darkness above.

It was almost nine o'clock now, and I knew that another carol-singing, of the Anglicans, was scheduled for then in a courtyard — of the Greek monastery — adjoining the Church of the Nativity. This ceremony, indeed, would be the only Protestant one connected with the church itself. In addition to it, and to the Y.M.C.A. party, there had been

— at seven o'clock — a small Presbyterian service at the Greek Shepherds' Fields, which I had not attended. Otherwise no Protestant services in English — catering to outsiders, that is — had been slated for Bethlehem on Christmas Eve or Christmas Day. Later a Lutheran divine, in Jerusalem, told me that from his Church's view the concentration on Bethlehem — so indulged in by the Catholics and the Eastern sects — was little better than relic-worship. He granted that emphasis on historic sites had value educationally — as fixing the Bible story in the mind — but beyond that he would not go. His was the Low Church position, however, as I worked it out later, and the Anglicans did not share it. They wished to mark the Nativity at its traditional site, and though they had a fine cathedral in Jerusalem — built in the eighteen nineties — they had no rights at the Church of the Nativity itself. They were on good terms with the Greeks, however, whose rights there were extensive, and the latter were letting them use their courtyard now.

The court was reached, I found, by a street along the church's southern side, and then by an archway; and once through this latter I saw that the place was already full of people holding candles. The sky was no longer hazy now, and the moon above was sharp and round. The Anglican Archbishop was standing on a platform at the court's east side, together with one of his canons and a Greek priest — the latter being evidence, it seemed, of a jealous guarding of rights at the church, by the different sects, of which I would learn more later. By the time I found a place amid the crowd the singing was under way — the carols were familiar ones, but often with unfamiliar British tunes. Between them came readings from Saints Luke and Matthew, and from the First Epistle General of Saint John.

When the carols were over I left the courtyard quickly, for I wanted to reach the Catholic service ahead of time. This was to be the great event of the evening, for which many people had come from faraway lands, and the Catholic pilgrims' office in Jerusalem had long been getting requests — far more than there were places — for admission to it. I had secured a ticket, but had been advised, nonetheless, to get there early if I hoped to see well. Therefore I headed directly for the church, even though this Catholic night service — there had also been a lesser one in the afternoon — was not due to start till half past ten.

My goal was not the Church of the Nativity proper, for the Catholics had no rights in most of that, as I was coming to learn. Rather it was their own church, called Saint Catherine's, which adjoins the main one on the north — where the Franciscan monastery also is. I journeyed round the great church establishment's edge — past the Greek monastery, past an Armenian monastery, past the church's own main door — till I reached Saint Catherine's door to its north; and there I found a scrum already in progress. A crowd was packed ahead of me densely, the people struggling to get in. Some were shouting angry words at each other, and some were disappearing as if sucked down by an undertow.

I didn't know what to do — for progress without violence seemed impossible — but luckily some policemen were laboring nearby, trying to control things, and one of them chanced to recognize me from the morning's motorcade. He called to me and got some of the others, and they took my arms and made a flying wedge before me, bearing me right to the open doorway and setting me down, miraculously, inside it. There I met the Franciscan father from whom I had got my reservation. "So you made it," he said with some surprise, and then he told me how to find my place. I was to sit in a balcony in the church's rear, and to get there I had to climb some stairs and cross a roof. This was rather an adventure, it turned out, and the roof was lovely in the moonlight.

I found a good seat in the balcony — front and center — though the place was filling up. It was assigned mainly to UN military men, I gathered, for several were there already, and more came later. These UN soldiers are quite a feature of Middle Eastern life now, and many of them are Christians — Europeans, Latin Americans, Canadians, etc. — so they had come in force to Jerusalem for the holiday. I nodded to those on hand and sat in my place.

Bells overhead were ringing, and the church was filling up, especially in the back, beneath us, where standing room was available on a first-come-first-served basis. I saw many Franciscan fathers down below — the Franciscans have charge of Saint Catherine's, as of most other Latin shrines in the Holy Land. I saw many Jordanian police as well — these were already becoming, in my mind, a part of the Christmas rites in Bethlehem (and I was, in fact, destined to see much more of them in this role, as the season went on and the Eastern Churches celebrated). The police were smart in their rough khaki uniforms and spiked helmets, and they were well rehearsed in this job of crowd control, doing it gently and effectively. Their main task at present was to ride herd in the back of the nave, where people were still jamming in for a few hours of standing. There were many Arab Legion soldiers among them, I noticed, and these kept their *kafiyahs* on, as the police did their helmets. The church's pews, more forward in the nave, were filled but scantily now, as the seats in them were reserved. But some people — including two rows of black-cowled nuns — were there already.

I sat at the balcony's rail and watched and waited; and toward half past ten the Patriarch entered the church, with many attendant prelates, priests, and choir-boys, in brilliant vestments. They proceeded to the sanctuary, at the church's far end — from my view — where they began performing Catholic matins. I shan't try to describe that ceremony beyond saying that the vestments, ritual, and music were as rich as any in my experience (and that the scene was made no less brilliant, incidentally, by the fact that I saw much of it through a lit-up chandelier). Meanwhile more and more people were joining the congregation, and being shown to their pews. But even after eleven there were many empty seats.

His Beatitude wore a crimson cape with ermine stole, and a crimson biretta, which he kept removing on occasion, over a crimson cap. Three other men in the sanctuary wore crimson, too, and later I heard that these were Monsignor Ryan, from Beirut, and two American bishops — Cuthbert O'Gara of New Jersey and Leo Smith of Buffalo. Another man in the sanctuary wore a white robe with the Holy Land cross (actually five crosses, a big one with four little ones in the corner spaces) marked in red on its breast; and he, I found out later, was a layman and a Knight of the Holy Sepulchre — a member of an order that helps, or used to help, preserve the Holy Places. Besides these there were many priests and choristers in the assemblage — dozens of them for most of the time, it seemed, though I never actually counted them. They sang the Divine Office, and the time went by.

At twenty minutes to twelve I heard some banging down

below me, and I saw that it was made by four *kawasses,* or liveried Arab servants. They had long staffs in their hands, quite plainly tipped with ferrules, and they were banging these on the flagstones with a slow rhythm. Meanwhile they were advancing up the aisle ahead of four men in dark clothes, who were (I later learned) the Roman Catholic consuls in Jerusalem, namely those of Italy, Belgium, Spain, and the Lebanon. The *kawasses* led them to the very front, put them in empty seats there, and withdrew.

Then in a few minutes came another banging, and *kawasses* appeared again, this time leading Jordanian notables. The banging of their staffs belonged to a common family of sounds in that region — the sound of metal on stone — for as one walks about in the Holy Land, one forever hears limestone being hit by pickaxes or chisels. The banging was impressive, too; it rang out through the church, with its slow-measured beat. And the *kawasses* led these other charges to the front and left them. After that the nave was wholly full. From my perch it looked like a field all planted with dark clothing — and here and there a bloom of scarlet, for a lady's hat or coat.

Just before midnight the bells pealed out above us — above the roof — and on the hour a solemn High Mass began, which would continue for some time. Early in it the Patriarch donned a mitre — large and yellow from my view, and no doubt brocaded. The choir-boys sang *Silent Night.* Then His Beatitude donned another mitre — the two were put on him and taken off repeatedly, by attendants. He stood before the altar, and priests waved a censer toward him. The mass went on. Then an electric star above the sanctuary lit up, and so did a neon Holy Land cross.

I stayed there in the balcony for some time longer, then felt I should have a look below. I went out across the roof, and the moon above was round and huge now, with a vast ring about it. The roof was wide and flat, and beyond it, on every hand, I saw moonlit, rolling country, silent in the night. Bells on the roof were ringing, though, and a big white flag, with a Holy Land cross in red, was flapping smartly.

I got down to ground level and went to the back of the nave; and the scene I found there was more lively, and more disordered, than I had reckoned on. The crowd was milling about and talking — it seemed more like a stock-exchange, almost, than a religious gathering — and later Catholic priests expressed disquiet to me over the way things had been conducted. They pointed out that many there had been Moslems, and that some of the rest had been Protestants; and they blamed their own church, too, for not making better arrangements. Yet personally I didn't mind the lack of devotional calm, for the life and warmth in the gathering were so appealing. I had sat up in the balcony for three or four hours, and meanwhile, unbeknownst to me, the people here below had gone through a lot. After struggling to enter the church's narrow door, then struggling to find places, they had stood — or sat if they were lucky — in fixed positions till their joints must certainly have ached and stiffened. Meanwhile the church had been filling up with incense, and warmth, and candlelight and other brilliance; and after twelve o'clock, apparently, a mood of relaxation had set in. Some of the congregation had left the church already, and some had taken to cruising around and talking with each other — nor was the talk always friendly, for I saw one man, a Jordanian, being led away in handcuffs, and I learned that he had been fighting.

I wandered around awhile, ranging farther afield. Outside the church's own entrance, in the Franciscan monastery or hostel, I discovered a room where refreshments were being sold. I bought a cup of tea, sat down to drink it, and found life being lived in that place, too — a pretty American girl, a tourist, had picked up a handsome Arab Legionnaire at some stage in the proceedings, and now the two were flirting over a snack.

I finished my cup and left the room again, finding a nearby cloister round a courtyard — still part of the Catholic establishment. I lingered there, wondering where to turn. I knew that soon — at about two o'clock in the schedule — His Beatitude was supposed to lead a procession to a grotto, under the actual Church of the Nativity, where Christ had, supposedly, been born; but I could see no hope of getting near that in the crowd. So I lingered indecisively.

Then suddenly — lo and behold — I heard a banging near me, and I looked up to see half a dozen *kawasses,* in a column of two's, coming at me into the cloister, through a door of the church. *Bang* . . . pause . . . *bang* . . . pause . . . *bang* . . . pause . . . *bang.* . . . Their ferrules were loud and commanding on the flags; and they came on slowly. I stepped aside as they got near, and they went past me. A double column of priests, singing and brightly vested, followed them. Then came the mitred Patriarch himself, surrounded by other prelates, and in his arms he bore an effigy of the Christ Child. It was specific in its imitation — flesh-colored, shiny, and waxen — like millions of dolls in America; and it lay in a manger, strawlined, as His Beatitude carried it on. Some canons held his train, and after them came the consuls and other notables, bearing candles; and I slipped quietly in among them.

We went round the cloister, but I was bewildered by the

singing and the lights, and I didn't note our course well. Then we passed through a door, and kept on, and suddenly I realized that we were in the Church of the Nativity itself. We were crossing its northern transept — ordinarily a domain, I was to learn, of the Armenians. The Church of the Nativity was darker — more shadowy overhead — than Saint Catherine's had been. It was also very crowded. There was a raised choir in front of us, and that was thronged with people watching; and others were packed beside us in the transept. They were kept out of our route only by two human fences, of Jordanian soldiers and policemen, who lined it and stood there clasping hands. Our procession went through this narrow lane, then came to the Grotto's stairs and started down. I followed along, and ended on one of the lowest steps, right near the Patriarch.

I looked around there. The Grotto's main body was long and narrow — the size, perhaps, of a smallish railway car. Our stairway led down, from the north, to the eastern end of this; and another — southern — stairway led down opposite. Both joined the Grotto at an angle — in such a way that the three parts, if seen from above, would make a Y in their layout. The stem of the Y, like its two arms — the stairways — was full of chanting priests now, and favored pilgrims and policemen. Only the region where they joined was clear, and that is where the Patriarch was standing. The scene around him was bright with candles and resonant with singing, and the air was warm and full of incense.

In front of His Beatitude, in the Y's east angle, a fourteen-pointed silver star was set in the floor. This marked the exact spot, traditionally, where Our Lord had been delivered. Now His Beatitude, amid chanting, knelt and symbolically laid the Baby's effigy there. Then he knelt again and passed a censer over it. Then he stepped back and spent some time in ritual — shedding his mitre, taking his crook from attendants, and so on. I saw now that he had a strong, ruddy, generous face, and that his beard was really light gray — just short of white.

The chanting continued, and two priests came forward to lay a cloth — brocaded — on the effigy. Then after a pause they raised the effigy and put it back in the manger. The chanting went on and on — now by one priest, now by many — and I gathered that the Gospel story was being sung, as well as enacted. Then priests took the manger, with the effigy inside, and set it on a nearby pedestal, where the real manger was thought, traditionally, to have stood. Then after a while the ritual there ended, and the return procession got under way, the effigy being left behind. The return was long, and we went slowly, but eventually we made it — back through the narrow lane amid the crowd — to Saint Catherine's again. And services went on there through the early hours.

I got to bed very late that night, in Jerusalem, and I slept late on Christmas Day. I did go to a morning service at the Anglican Cathedral, but I did not return to Bethlehem for a pilgrimage the Catholics staged, that afternoon, to their Shepherds' Fields. I just let the occasion trail off, and in most countries that would have been the end of it. But in the Holy Land it was just the beginning, for the Eastern Churches hadn't done a thing yet.

The GReek ChRiSTMAS

In Bethlehem Christmas comes not once a year, but thrice. First there is the Western Christmas we all know. Then there is a second one, on January seventh, often called the Greek Orthodox Christmas in the Holy Land, though it is actually observed by the Syrian, Coptic, and Ethiopian Churches, too. Then finally there is an Armenian Christmas, of the Armenian Church alone, on January nineteenth. It also works out that the Western Epiphany falls on the Greeks' Christmas Eve, and the Greek Epiphany on the Armenians' Christmas, a situation that adds dramatic rhythm, at least, to the season — the Armenians have no separate Epiphany, and thus avoid what might be an anticlimax from the dramatic view (if one may speak of such a thing in this connection). These differences cry out, of course, for an explanation, and when in the Holy Land I sought one.

"It is rather complicated," I was told by one scholar, a Western Protestant. "In part, at least, the question hinges on the Epiphany. In the Western Church, as you know, the Epiphany is largely concerned with the visit of the

30

wise men, but in the Eastern it is equally concerned, and always was, with Christ's baptism and the start of His ministry — with His temptation, for instance, and with the marriage at Cana in Galilee, where He performed His first miracle. Up to the fourth century of the Christian era the Epiphany was the big occasion — aside from Easter and the Resurrection — and it centered on these things. Other early events in the Gospel story, including the birth, were often celebrated then, too, but the birth was not marked separately. It was in Rome, and in the West generally, that the idea of marking the birth as such originally grew popular; and the date of December twenty-fifth grew popular there, too — the reasons for choosing it are obscure, but at least they had little to do with the historical date itself, which was not known. Anyway once this practice, of holding Christmas on December twenty-fifth, was established in Rome, it spread quickly through the Empire and beyond. Soon all the Eastern Churches took it up, though the Armenians dropped it again before long and went back to the old single Epiphany. With this one exception — of the Armenians — the whole Church then observed Christmas in unison for more than a thousand years, until the calendar reform of Gregory the Thirteenth, in 1582. Ever since then the Western Church has followed the Gregorian calendar, while the Eastern has stuck to the Julian, at least here in the Holy Land; and as a result there has been a gap — gradually widening — between their Christmases, which in this century amounts to thirteen days. That is why the Greeks celebrate the event on January seventh, which they, of course, call December twenty-fifth. And the Armenians do it on the nineteenth, which they call the sixth. They celebrate all the events connected with the old Epiphany then — the birth, the flight into Egypt, the massacre of the innocents, the baptism, the temptation, the marriage at Cana, and so on — though the day is often thought of here as the Armenian Christmas alone, by analogy with the other Christmases."

This statement pretty well covered the date question for me — my other researches only confirmed it and added a few details around the edges. An Armenian priest, for one thing, told me that outside the Holy Land his Church follows the Gregorian, not the Julian, calendar. "For instance, in America," he said, "we celebrate our Christmas on your January sixth — or rather we do it on the nearest Sunday to that, so our people can get away from their jobs."

Another Armenian told me that the Roman Church had moved its emphasis to December twenty-fifth, way back in early times, so as to blanket out, or appropriate, a Mithraic sun-worshipping festival on that date, which had been ingrained in the people's habits. "Our Church finally decided," he explained, "that the Romans were identifying Jesus with the sun, and we felt this was idolatrous. That's why we gave the separate Christmas up."

(I also read, by the way, that December twenty-fifth had been a feast-day in Britain long before Christianity had reached there. But I found no hint that this had influenced the Church in its choice of a date — however much it may have blended extraneous items, like mistletoe, into the festivities.)

Having taken in the Latin Christmas, I was resolved to stay on for the Greek and Armenian ones to learn something about them, and about the Churches concerned. On this program the next main item, ritualistically, was the Greeks' procession from Jerusalem to Bethlehem on the morning of January sixth (Gregorian), their Christmas

Eve. I meant to watch this — or rather its arrival at the Bethlehem end — but earlier that day I wanted to see another event: the crossing of Greek-Christian Arabs from Israel to Jordan for the holiday. Normally no crossing is allowed from Israel to Jordan — except on the part of diplomats, UN officials, and the like — but exceptions are made, at the different Christmases and Easters, for many of Israel's Christian community. This community, numbering forty-five thousand, consists almost wholly of Arabs, and its members can be Greek-Christian Arabs, Latin-Christian Arabs, Syrian-Christian Arabs — or, for that matter, Anglican- or Lutheran-Christian Arabs — depending on their Church affiliation. I knew that something like seventeen hundred Arabs had come over for the Latin Christmas, and that a roughly equal number was expected for the Greek; and so early on the sixth, I arrived at the "Mandelbaum Gate," which is the official place of crossing.

It isn't a gate, really. It is just a section of a street, in Jerusalem's north suburbs, where the truce line between the countries happens to fall. On the Jordan side of this line the street has yellow stone walls across it, laid out in a baffle formation so that cars can serpentine through them, but bullets cannot. Ordinarily one is not allowed beyond those walls, but as a journalist I could pass them this morning. On their far side the road slopes downward to a no-man's-land and then to Israel; and today a tent, with open sides, was pitched near the crest of this, in Jordan territory. Underneath it stood several small wooden tables with Jordanian policemen waiting by them. To the tables, from the Israel direction, led lanes of ropes on stakes, and some of these were full of queues already, while others were empty.

"The different tables," a policeman told me, "are for

people from different towns on the other side, like Jerusalem, Acre, Jaffa, Nazareth, and Haifa. The people from
the nearest towns are here already — and their lanes are
full — but those from Nazareth, for instance, won't come
till later, when the morning bus gets down from there."

The crossers in their lines were waiting, often, to see
close relatives after a long separation; but they were standing patiently as Asians do. They wore their best clothing,
apparently, though much of it was none too good. The
men had Western suits on as a rule, and the women bright-
colored overcoats. Most of them held suitcases or cloth
bags, and one woman carried flowers.

"They come with nothing," the policeman said, "but
they will take back lots — especially things to eat, as food
is cheaper here. They are allowed to bring only one pound
in currency from Israel, but their relatives here will give
them more — will even sell some jewelry, perhaps — so
they can buy what they want. Many of them will go back
loaded down — come here tomorrow and you can see
them. They'll be going through till six o'clock then.
They've been coming here since six this morning, and they
have thirty-six hours till they must be back."

"What happens," I asked, "if they try to stay on longer?"

"Oh, they often do," he answered, "but then we find
them. Through their relatives. They must give the address of relatives in Jordan beforehand, you see, or they
can't come in. And they are easy to trace that way."

The lines were moving slowly up to the tables, where
paper-work was going on. The crossers were handing in
their Israeli identification cards, the policeman explained
to me, and getting Jordanian passes in return — on the way
back they would simply reverse that process.

"We stop some of them here," he went on. "About five

or ten per cent of those who come. Because we have found them on our blacklists after their names have been sent over. It seems that the other side turns many back, too — at least there are many who fail to come after their names have been sent and we have O.K.'d them. We believe the police over there have stopped them because they are related to army officers here, or something like that."

"It must be a great disappointment," I said, "to get this far and then be stopped."

"Yes," he answered. "Of course we feel for them when we turn them back on this side. Yet we can't help it. They are on the blacklist. We are afraid. Perhaps they are spies or something."

The policeman was restrained in his speech, yet he obviously, if tacitly, placed the blame for all such misfortunes on Israel. And I assumed — and later confirmed — that the Israelis, just across the line, would be placing it on Jordan. Where it really belonged — except on human nature in general — I did not know, and at the moment I was more interested in the poignancy of the line-crossing, anyway, than in the merits of this Arab-Israeli dispute. As time went on, though, I was going to find that dispute rather like those within the Christian Church. The Arab-Israeli trouble has many facets, but not the least of them is the religious one — the ancient rivalry between Islam and Judaism. During my Christmas-going, and my related inquiries, I was to find this rivalry foreshadowed, in spirit, by the rivalry between the Christian sects — and also, historically speaking, by that between Islam and Christianity as a whole.

But these thoughts would come later — now I was only watching the crossers cross. They could not meet their relatives near the tent, it seemed, for the latter were still in their purgatory in the no-man's-land — to leave it they had to continue up the slope and enter a large buff-lime-stone building, near the baffle walls, where they would go through customs. Then they would pass out on the other side, and be wholly in Jordan and be met. So I went round to that side after a while, to have a look. There was an empty lot there, carpeted with the hard dusty soil so common in Palestine, and on this a throng of people was wait-ing, and milling around. They were kept from the lime-stone building itself by a barrier, partly of barbed wire; and many were leaning against this, watching expectantly. It so happened that the newcomers would round a corner, usually, before they could be seen, and as each did so, or-dinarily, some members of the crowd would call out, or clap, and wave excitedly. They would smile all over as the newcomer responded, and they would struggle toward him — or perhaps they would point to another place, in the rear, where he should meet them; for the crowd by the barrier was dense and hard to push through. Then when they came together there would be tears and hugs and kisses — between men as well as women, in the Arab manner. It was like school-children coming home, in the West, for Christmas, but more demonstrative.

Some crossers were not met, immediately, by anyone, and these looked sad by comparison. They trailed off on their lonesome through the crowd. Yet in some cases, at least, the non-meeting must have come from faulty timing, as the whole occasion had an air of approximation over it, of Asian casualness. The crowd seemed ready to stay there all morning, if need be, and lots of hawkers were on hand to exploit this fact. Some were selling chewing-gum, some candy, some apples or bananas, and some eggs. At least three stands were selling quoit-like Arab buns with sesame-seeds on them. And a coffee-vendor was threading his way through the multitude, bearing a huge brass pot and clinking two small cups together, as a cry. All in all, it was a pleasant, festive scene; and warm sunlight slanted down on it in the morning.

I left there soon, though, and got in a taxi and headed south for Bethlehem. I traveled the same route as I had on the Latin Christmas Eve, but now I was ahead of the Patriarch concerned, not in his retinue.

This duplication of patriarchs in the Holy Land, of course, was another thing that called for an explanation, and since the Latin Christmas I had been rounding one up. In the Church's early centuries, I had learned, there came in time to be five patriarchs — at Rome, Constantinople, Jerusalem, Alexandria, and Antioch — and these were its highest authorities. The Patriarch of Rome was somewhat higher than the others, though — by virtue, at least in part, of the apostolic succession from Saint Peter, who had been martyred in that city — and in time he developed into the Pope we know of. In Western eyes he came to seem the center of all Christendom, though in Eastern ones he remained just another, somewhat bigger patriarch — *"primus inter pares"* was the phrase, or "first among equals." His four colleagues continued undisturbed by his growing status until the Crusades, which brought Catholic power eastward.

Until just before Crusader times Jerusalem continued to have a resident Patriarch — a single one — and he was Greek, and close to Constantinople, because the Byzantine Empire ruled both places in the fourth, fifth, and sixth centuries. In the seventh, however, the Arabs conquered the Holy Land, and in the tenth — after a long relative calm

— their regime began persecuting the Christians severely. The Patriarch fled to Cyprus as a result; the Crusaders went into action; and when in time they set up their Latin kingdom in Jerusalem, they installed a Latin Patriarch as well, replacing the absent Orthodox one. The latter returned, though, after 1187, when Saladin reconquered Jerusalem and launched a new and gentler Arab foreign policy. Yet the Latin Patriarchate continued to exist, and thus there came to be two.*

And two there still are, religious institutions being so long-lasting in the Holy Land. I found that their roles are somewhat different, though, as I inquired into them. The Latin Patriarch, I was told by a Franciscan father, belongs to the second highest rank among those Church princes who have regional authority — he is below the Pope, that is, but above the archbishops and the bishops (his rank compared with the various cardinals is ill-defined). He also has as colleagues three other Catholic patriarchs — of Venice, Lisbon, and India — whose posts have little to do with the early Church.

Exalted as are these Catholic patriarchs, of course, they are still just part of the rigid hierarchy under the Vatican. The Greek Patriarch in Jerusalem, on the other hand, seems to be much like his predecessors — an independent ruler, albeit somewhat lesser than the Ecumenical Patriarch in Constantinople (now called Istanbul by the Turks, but not the Greeks). The Greek patriarchs, like the Latin, have also acquired new colleagues with the march of time, for as the Orthodox Church has spread in Europe it has established *national* Patriarchates there, which now exist in

---

* But from the fall of the Crusader kingdom till 1847 the Latin Patriarch actually lived in Rome, not Jerusalem. During this period it was the Franciscans who looked out for Latin interests in the Holy Land.

Russia, Yugoslavia, Romania, and Bulgaria. These too are largely autonomous — "autocephalous" is the technical term — as, for that matter, are certain Orthodox archbishoprics, like that of Cyprus; for the Eastern system has never copied the centralization of the Western.

Besides being nearly autonomous in the Holy Land, anyway, the Greek Patriarch also happens to have the biggest Christian flock there; and today — when I reached Bethlehem — I found it out in force to greet him, though no doubt the crowd included many others. The sky above the little town was blue again. The day before I had seen the last of the old moon — which had been so full on the Western Christmas — up there in it, looking like a silver fingernail. Now too, of course, the sun was shining brightly — the drought had not abated — and it fell like gold on the tawny buildings. When I reached Manger Square I saw that the Catholics' angel had been removed from the big pine tree and that a Greek banner, with a picture of the Nativity, had been put up instead. Otherwise the scene was much as it had been — with lights strung over the Square, bunting wrapped on the tree-trunk, and so on. The place was clotted now with bits of crowd — not yet full up — and the Arab Legion band was playing popular tunes, including *Shish Kebab* and *Nights of Lebanon,* which then were hits in the Arab world.

From Manger Square the vista is unbroken — across the intervening plaza — to the Church of the Nativity. Outwardly this structure bears little resemblance to formal churches as we know them — rather it is like a medieval fort, surrounded by great walls of limestone masonry. It is, in fact, a large compound, mainly roofed over, and besides the principal church it embraces Saint Catherine's

— of the Roman Catholics — along with the attendant Greek, Armenian, and Catholic monasteries.

There are courtyards, too, and even gardens, within the compound, connected with these monasteries; and below the ground there are several limestone caves, including the Grotto of the Nativity itself. The walls round the church were built mainly as a defense, against the Arabs, and they are mightily thick. "The walls of our monastery take up more room than the rooms do," an Armenian priest once told me, when showing me round; and he added that no changes could be made without permission from the other Churches — so jealously, and rigidly, are the rights in the whole establishment defined.

This Armenian monastery is the first part of the church compound that one reaches when coming from Manger Square — it juts out from the rest like a panhandle, toward the town. If you continue east you have it on your right, or southern hand; and meanwhile you cross the big plaza, paved too in limestone, that leads to the main church door. The plaza is the size of several tennis courts, but the door itself is tiny, and if you continue through it you must bow your head. It wasn't always that way — the doorway once was vast and monumental, but it was later twice diminished, for defense and also — I have been told — to keep Moslems from taking their animals inside. The outlines of the older entrances can still be seen in the masonry — first a big flat-linteled one, then a smaller pointed arch; and then, mortared up inside this, the present tiny oblong. Traces of all sorts can be seen in the church, indeed, from the Crusader period and the Byzantine as well. It is a whole course of archeology, while still in use.

Now on this sunny morning, while waiting for the Patriarch, I wandered back and forth in Manger Square and in the plaza, which is sometimes called the church's forecourt. The pipes and drums of the Arab Legion came and played in the forecourt awhile. They sounded good — better than most of the other bagpipe outfits, I thought — Sikh, Gurkha, and the like — that the British army has left behind in Asia. They marched back and forth through themselves, and the drum-major tossed his baton high. Then the pipes withdrew, and the Legion's brass band, also good, came on again. The crowd kept thickening, and as I looked around I noted the Greek Patriarchate's flag above the church; it is white and bears a red cross as well as the monogram ₤, for τάφος or tomb — meaning the Holy Sepulchre in Jerusalem, to which the Patriarchate is attached. The red-and-white flag waved prettily against the blue sky, atop the yellow building.

At about nine-thirty, while standing idly there, I heard a familiar sound nearby — of metal periodically hitting stone — and I looked in that direction to see a small procession coming at me, led by two *kawasses* in livery. The latter struck the flagstones with their staffs, and behind them came a little group of priests, wearing black caps and rather dingy vestments — I heard the complaint, indeed, from a nearby camera-wielding tourist, that they weren't much good for color photographs. The procession was, I realized, a delegation of the Syrian Christians, and it continued across the forecourt, banging the while, till it reached the little church door and went inside.

I hung around some more, and before very long I heard another banging — this time by three *kawasses* — and a delegation of the Coptic Church appeared. It included — I learned from a bystander — an archbishop up from Egypt; and on their heads its members wore *tarbooshes* with small black turbans bound around them. That group, too, banged on across the forecourt and entered the church; and then off to one side, in its rear, I saw two Ethiopian priests, who were walking along unobtrusively, without *kawasses* or other display. They were tall and dignified — though they were young, and their beards were sparse — but they were not especially vested. They wore street clothing, of black robes and black cylindrical hats; and they told me, when I spoke to them, that this was in fact their Christmas Eve, of course, but that they would not celebrate it in the church because they had no rights there. They were just informal visitors, they said; and as such they, too, crossed the court and disappeared.

These arrivals were only a sideshow, however — if, again, we may speak in terms of spectacles — and it was in Manger Square itself that the crowd kept building up, for the Greek procession was due there at eleven. I went back there — picking my way through hawkers of postcards, candy, shoeshines, and the like — and in the Square I met a policeman I had come to know, who asked me to a nearby building for some coffee. The building belonged normally, I think, to the District Officer — the town's administrator — but today it was a headquarters, or at least the downstairs was, for the police and Arab Legion.

The policeman took me to a back room, sat me at a table there, and served me a cup of Turkish coffee, thick and sweetish. The band of the Legion — now not performing — had its instruments stacked near us, and five of the bandsmen sat at another table, playing cards. I asked my host if the police problem was greater today, or less, than on the Western Christmas. "It's about the same," he said. "The crowd is the same size, pretty much, and our duties, too, are much the same." He added that the Bethlehem police had been reinforced, on both occasions, by detachments from other Jordan towns, like Amman, Jerusalem, and Hebron.

After drinking the coffee, and taking my leave, I stood awhile on the steps outside the headquarters, watching the Square. As I did so, a column of other police marched out past me. In number they were about equal to an infantry platoon, and they cleared the center of the Square and formed lines to keep the crowd outside this. Soon after they were set, a man driving a donkey penetrated to them, from the crowd's outskirts, but he was turned back; and from then on the place ceased to be a route for traffic.

The crowd was almost wholly Arab, I saw — there were some Western tourists about, but much fewer than on the Latin Christmas. Nor, as I verified later, were there many Eastern Christians from outside of Palestine. Easter is a more important feast than Christmas for the Orthodox, and hordes of visitors from, say, Cyprus pour in then to Jerusalem. But Christmas they leave to the local people; and the Greek Christmas, furthermore, is more local than the Latin, as the Orthodox is, pre-eminently, the local Church.

Toward half past ten a very tall man, in a *kafiyah* and a smart gray Western overcoat, arrived in a car. He got down, entered the District Officer's building, and soon appeared at a balcony on its upper floor. He was, I learned, a man named Hassan Bey, the Muhafez, or Military Governor, of Jerusalem and nearby points, and I was to see more of him before the Christmases were over. He was himself a Moslem, and a very devout one, reputedly — he came from the Hejaz, the holy region down near Mecca — but he was also a civil official, and as such was there to represent the government. He must have been an old man, for I learned that he had served under the Turks, and later the

British, in the Palestine police. But he looked fresh and vigorous enough — and also calm and stately — as he stood there on the balcony.

At twenty minutes to eleven I saw a procession coming from the Church of the Nativity — one or two hundred yards away. It moved slowly and was led by a boy in purple, with a big silver cross. Behind him came many priests, wearing black cylindrical hats, black beards, and black skirts beneath brocaded robes — these last were brilliant and elaborate; and their general hue, as seen in the distance, was peach or apricot. Eight or ten other boys were in the company, I soon made out — they, too, wore purple, and they carried standards and banners.

In time they all reached the center of the Square, and they stood there waiting, informally. A rug was laid down, and the smoke of sandalwood arose from censers. From my perch on the steps I moved over near the priests, on the Square's other side. They were standing there at ease, holding crosses, censers, Bibles, and other instruments, done in gold and silver, and richly jeweled. Their robes were brocaded with gold thread — or so it seemed — on a background near to crimson. Not all the priests were vested thus, however, I noted now — perhaps two dozen were, but a dozen more were dressed in black. They all wore long hair, besides their beards. I got whiffs of the sandalwood as I stood there gazing at them. It had a sweet tang in the crystal air, and its smoke was white in the sunshine.

A middle-aged, plumpish man appeared in a swallowtail coat, and I learned that he was the District Officer of Bethlehem. Then the Mayor of Bethlehem — a lesser official in a black suit — appeared as well. A number of other Arabs — portly and eminent-looking — were on the scene now, too. One of them — he wore a *kafiyah* and a brown *burnoose* or robe — was pointed out to me as the leader of an Arab refugee colony near Bethlehem. Another, in a business suit, was pointed out as a doctor in Jerusalem and a pillar of the orthodox Moslem community. The priests themselves were Greek by birth, yet as they stood there waiting they chatted in Arabic with these notables.

Just after eleven, bells on the church rang out. Then a boy-scout band, with beating drums, came marching through us from the opposite — the western — direction. Then mounted policemen, with lances and pennants, came following on their heels, but when they reached the crowded Square they parted and went round it. And by that time His Beatitude's car itself — a black sedan — was in our midst, and it had stopped, and His Beatitude got down from it. He was a small man, imperious in bearing, with a strong aquiline nose and a full gray beard resting on his chest. He wore a veil over his cylindrical hat, and his vestments were gorgeous in red, purple, green, and gold — in jewels and brocades. I could not keep him in sight, though, because of the crowd, which was milling about; and presently it all began to move. A captain of police led off the procession; then the Patriarch followed with his chanting priests and choir-boys; then a line of other police, in khaki, with their spiked khaki helmets, brought up the rear — they were clasping hands to hold the crowd back. His Beatitude had a large cross in his left hand and a small one in his right — both glistening richly — and he moved the right one, in repeated passes, as he walked. He walked on slowly, reached the church door, and disappeared inside.

The door was so small that the crowd, behind him, went through it like sand in an hourglass. I was delayed a long time, but eventually I made it. Then I crossed a shallow narthex, or entrance hall, and after that I was in the nave of the old church itself. In shape it was a good deal like the nave of the Catholic church, Saint Catherine's, where I had spent the Western Christmas Eve, but its atmosphere was different. It had less light; less organization (no pews, for instance); more spaciousness; more dramatic quality; and also, of course, more age. It was, indeed, one of the oldest big churches in Christendom, having been built by order of Justinian, the Byzantine emperor, in the sixth century A.D. (and on the ruins, even then, of an earlier church, or basilica, built by Constantine and his mother around 325). As I stood there, the Christmas-goers still kept dribbling into the church, behind me, but most of them hurried on up the nave to the other end, where there was a raised choir, like a stage. Up there a crowd was thickening, on and around the choir; and a service, I gathered, was about to start. There was a rich yellow glow above it all, from lamps and candles, and from burnished icons on a screen beyond them.

I refrained awhile from going there; I lingered in the back. The broken, random crowd flowed on away from me, on the open flagstone floor, while above it — in the vasty space — sunbeams sloped down from high clerestory windows. The walls below those windows, and around and above them, were dull in tone, but here and there small golden patches shone quietly in them — remains, these were, of mosaics, some Byzantine and some from Crusader times, but all done by workmen in the Byzantine tradition. There were also remains of frescoes, seen now as dim bits of color — pinks and greens.

I had been reading about these works. Twice in history, I had gathered — in Byzantine times (say around 600) and in Crusader times (say 1100) — the church's whole walls must have shone forth brilliantly; but now there was just this echo. The Turks, ruling Bethlehem for four centuries, after 1500, had forbidden repairs to the walls, because, being Moslems, they had thought the pictures idolatrous. The jealousy between the sects had helped to block the work, too, and neglect had had its way. Only fragments of mosaic were left now, and some were streaked with plaster running down.

The nave as a whole was stately, though. High above was a wood-raftered ceiling. Then the walls came down on either side, past the mosaics and the clerestory, to colonnades that ran along their bottoms, screening aisles. Between these the big wide limestone floor, with the crowd moving on it, led up to the choir. The people seemed insignificant in scale, and one felt that no matter what their numbers they could never dominate the church. It was too grand for that — too monumental, durable, and old.

In time I followed the crowd up, and there was a thick press in the choir. Policemen and *kawasses* were moving people round there, and maintaining alleys through them — and sometimes helping the more favored, substantial-looking ones advance to better places. The Patriarch and priests were off the scene now, and I think they were in the Grotto underneath us — for soon the banging of *kawasses* was heard near one of its entrances, and His Beatitude came into view behind them. He moved, by a path in the crowd, to the choir's center, before the icon screen, and there in due course — and amid due ritual and singing — he was seated; and the crowd began coming up to kiss his hand.

The people were eager, and hard to restrain. They *would* push forward, and between them they seemed to have all the usual motives for this — devotion, that is, and curiosity, and desire to be seen (not to mention desire to take photographs). Mothers would rush up eagerly with little children, to give them a look. The police were gentle with the people on the whole, but tough when they had to be. Meanwhile the services went on, with lovely singing; and incense rose along with *Kyrie eleisons.* The ritual had the tall icon screen as a background. On it were many Russian icons — gifts from the devout in Czarist times — and these gleamed with white and yellow metal.

The choir and the icon screen (and the sanctuary beyond it) are absolute preserves of the Orthodox Church, I had been learning — no other sect is allowed to use them. The big long nave — behind me as I faced the screen — belongs mainly to the Orthodox, too, with a few reservations. And besides these parts the building has northern and southern side-arms or transepts — for, like most other churches, it is laid out in a cross. The northern transept, I knew now, belongs mainly to the Armenians, though again with some reservations; and the southern, like the choir, belongs to the Greeks, with the odd exception that the Moslems, non-Christians, sometimes pray in it. This custom was started by the Caliph Omar, when he conquered the Holy Land for Islam in 638. He entered the church respectfully — since Moslems, too, venerate Jesus as a prophet — and he prayed in the south transept because it was the nearest part to Mecca. Ever since then pious Moslems have prayed there on occasions — policemen on duty in the church are said to do it sometimes.

Today, when I had seen enough of the service in the choir, I went out through that south transept. A Greek priest was selling candles there, and many Greek nuns, in black robes and black velvet caps, were seated on benches by the walls — the walls themselves being liberally, indeed crowdedly, hung with Greek and Russian paintings. I looked around there awhile; then I left all the church's life and color — and the singing — for sunny outdoor Bethlehem.

I ate a picnic lunch in my taxi, which I had kept the while. I read and rested there. Then I took a stroll round the sunlit Square, which was more or less empty now, but still festive — a child in a grotesque mask, for one thing, came rushing at me as I walked. Later I went back to the church and the fray inside. The place had been filling up nicely with incense smoke, and the sunbeams in the nave were silvery — less golden than they had been. Some scattered people were standing in the nave, too, and an Arab guide there offered to show me round, but I declined. I went up to the choir, and there was a big congregation on (or in) it, mainly of women. His Beatitude was seated as before, and priests were singing, *Kyrie eleison*.

I knew that the Syrians' Christmas service should be on now (they having spent the past few hours, according to the program, in retirement in the Armenian monastery). I looked for them and found them, in the north transept. They numbered half a dozen priests, a few choir-boys, and some layman singers, the latter wearing black gowns over mufti. They all were gathered at an altar in the transept's corner, and they were chanting, although the Greeks — very near them — were chanting, too. The Syrian priests were bearded like the Greek ones, but instead of cylindrical hats they wore black knitted caps or cowls, with tiny white or yellow crosses embroidered on them. They were less grand or pretentious than the Greeks — less rich, perhaps.

They were holding their little service in Armenian territory, and because of this an Armenian priest was standing there — to see, as I found out later, that they did nothing they were not entitled to do. The priest was a young
man and dark, and he wore the impressive formal street
attire of Armenian celibates — its main feature is a black
peaked hood of watered silk; this falls down over the
shoulders rather like a Ku Klux hood, but is cut away to
show the face and beard. The Armenian stood there
quietly, and a khaki-clad policeman stood beside him —
disputes, it seems, do sometimes rise in these juxtapositions
of the sects; and the Jordan authorities must then take a
position in them.

I stood watching the little service, and as I did so a
young Syrian priest — thin and intense, with a long black
beard — accosted me. "Those are Syriac priests," he told
me eagerly in English. "They are singing the Gospel story,
and singing it in the language used by Christ." The place
was not a good one for pursuing this subject, but I was interested, and I learned that I could find the young priest
later in Jerusalem, which I resolved to do.

Right near the Syrians a stairway went down, to the
Grotto of the Nativity itself — these were the stairs I had
traversed on the Latin Christmas. Around them a semicircular stairhead was cut in the limestone floor — it dated
from the time of Justinian — and from it the steps slanted
down beneath the choir. I walked down them now. No
service was in progress in the Grotto, but a few people
were there, some praying. The Grotto's walls, and those of
the two stairways leading down to it, were hung with
drapes. The whole place was warm and bright from candles,
and from oil-lamps — two dozen or more — suspended
from the ceiling.

I sat down on a bench, by the north wall, and watched and rested for a while. Opposite me, by the supposed place where Jesus had been cradled, a Franciscan monk was praying. The effigy of the Christ Child lay there, too, in its straw-lined portable manger, just as the Roman Catholics had left it on their Christmas Eve. (Later today, according to the program, they would remove it again, as part of their Epiphany service.) Off to my left, as I sat, the silver star lay in the floor at the spot where the Nativity itself, supposedly, had taken place. The star had a big round hole in it, through which could be seen the living limestone — the floor itself was of masonry — and from time to time a worshipper would enter the Grotto, by a stairway, and kneel to kiss this rock. Other worshippers knelt nearby, praying, and still others — mere visitors, perhaps — stood chatting or idling in the background.

Among these last I chanced to spy the Arab guide who had approached me earlier, in the nave, and on a hunch I asked him to tell me about the Grotto. He was glad to do it — glad of any business — and he did it well, and truthfully to judge by my later reading.

"There was no church here before the fourth century, you know," he said. "The cave was outside Bethlehem's limits then, in a grove that was sacred to Adonis. Pagan rites were held there. Some say the Romans had started this practice, to help in their suppression of Christianity. No doubt they had, but anyway things changed when Constantine legalized the faith in 313. Soon after that his mother, the Empress Helena, came to the Holy Land as a pilgrim — she was very devout, you know. She found the Holy Sepulchre in Jerusalem and had a church built there, and she found this Grotto and had one built over it too. Of course Constantine helped her. It is said that he was building up Christianity to hold the empire together, but her motives are thought to have been more purely devout. Of course she was an intelligent woman, and she may have seen that definite shrines, authentic or not, were needed for the new religion — she may not have been too careful, I mean, about the evidence for the sites she chose. Anyway this Grotto did become a great shrine after she had singled it out."

Later in the fourth century, the guide went on, Saint Jerome came to Bethlehem from Italy, to write the Latin Vulgate, his translation of the Bible. According to one tradition he did the work in another cave beneath the church. There are several such caves, I learned, though we couldn't go into them that day — in another of them, tradition says, the bodies of the innocent babies were placed, after Herod had them killed.

"The pilgrims flocked in here," the guide said, "at the time of Saint Jerome and later, and Bethlehem grew and prospered. Constantine's church was destroyed, though, in the reign of Justinian — probably by the Samaritans, from up north of Jerusalem, who rebelled then, briefly, against the Christian-Byzantine yoke. Justinian rebuilt the church, but the Persians came close to destroying it again, in 614. They conquered Palestine then, and ruined many Christian shrines, but in the Church of the Nativity they found a mural of the three wise men — dressed up, appropriately, like Persians — and for that reason they spared the place. Thus the church and Grotto have come down pretty much intact since Justinian, though minor changes have been made throughout the centuries."

The guide began pointing to various features from the different periods — a Byzantine mosaic above the Star of the Nativity, for instance, and some Crusader marble columns near the stairs. He talked quietly, and we moved about discreetly, because of the worshippers coming and going there, in the warm and flame-lit atmosphere.

"For several centuries," the guide continued, "a rivalry has existed between the Churches, and now their rights in the Grotto are strictly defined. Only the Greeks, Armenians, and Roman Catholics have continuous rights here. The Copts and Syrians will hold services here this evening, but only on sufferance and under supervision — and they may not enter the Grotto, officially, during the rest of the year. As for the three Churches who do hold rights, the Latins control the manger, and the Greeks and Armenians share control over the altar at the end there, above the Star of the Nativity. The vessels and pictures that each may have on the altar are strictly limited.

"The lamps on the ceiling are portioned out, too — the Greeks, Armenians, and Latins each control one third of them. The floor beneath us is a no-man's-land, however." He pointed downward, to simple flagstones, worn smooth. "If a lamp falls on the floor," he said, "no priest from any of the Churches may clean the spot up, for that might constitute a claim to rights there. The only one who may clean it is the Moslem policeman on duty in the church. He must be sent for."

Strange as was this tale, it was all borne out by what I later read. And the guide went on. In the nineteenth century, he said, the diplomatic rivalry between France and Russia found expression in the Grotto — the French pushing the Latin claims there, and the Russians the Greek ones, before the corrupt and pressionable Turks. During that phase the silver Star of the Nativity disappeared one night — not to be found again — and this was among the causes of the Crimean War. Later a new star was given by the Turkish Sultan.

And the guide pointed out another distinguished contribution in the Grotto — asbestos-treated hangings given in 1873 by Marshal MacMahon, the French president, to replace an earlier set destroyed by burning. Nor did I wonder at the burning, as I watched the candles blazing in that tiny place.

I paid the guide, thanked him, and went back upstairs. The Greek service in the choir was drawing to an end now — it had been on for nearly four hours. Soon the little, forceful-looking Patriarch arose and left, ceremoniously. But the congregation, by and large, remained, and they shifted to the choir's northern edge, which looked down, from its higher level, on the northern transept.

"All the people here are waiting," an Arab woman told me. "They are waiting for the little baby."

I waited, too. The Syrians had left the transept now — it was half past three — but a crowd was there, and soon a number of policemen came and joined them. The police opened a door in the transept's northwest corner — giving on Saint Catherine's — and then they began lining up to make a double fence, with a narrow lane between them, leading from there to the Grotto. They were getting ready for the Catholic Epiphany procession, which would follow the same route as the Christmas one, twelve days earlier.

I had walked in some bewilderment in that Christmas procession, but now I could see the layout of the route more clearly. Schematically the lane was much like other diplomatic corridors — the Polish Corridor, for instance. It led through Armenian sovereignty, in effect, and it was needed

as a way to get the Catholics from their base, Saint
Catherine's, to their objective, the Grotto, and back again.
The Armenians had agreed to this — much as the Germans, no doubt, had once agreed to let the Poles come
through — but their agreement had a legalistic sharpness
to it: even without the police, as I confirmed later on,
the Catholics were not allowed to take a step outside the
corridor. Two or three authorities told me, even, that a
priest had once been killed for doing so, though I didn't
find this in the written records.

The police took pains now, anyway, to get their lines
all straight, and meanwhile the crowd thickened up outside them. Then from Saint Catherine's a banging of *kawasses* sounded, and the procession came slowly into sight.
The *kawasses* were followed by priests in a long double file
— vested in white and gold, they were, and bearing candles
and singing. They moved through the sombre crowd like
a white river through brown banks. Then in time the procession's main personage appeared, though it was not the
Patriarch this time. It was another Catholic prelate, the
Custos of the Holy Land — the head of the Franciscan
order there, which oversees the Holy Places.

("His Paternity" was the honorific pronoun, incidentally
— His Paternity the Custos. His Paternity the Custos was
a lesser figure than His Beatitude the Patriarch — indeed
His Beatitude Alberto Gori, the present Patriarch, had
been His Paternity the Custos as a younger man. Like
Alberto Gori, too, the present Custos, Alberto Polidori,
was an Italian — "The Custos is always an Italian," an
American priest was to tell me later; "it's one of those
things.")

The Custos was a tall man, with a beard and spectacles,
and now he wore a gold-and-whitish mitre. Two pages

followed him, and then came notables in business suits. They marched on slowly, and in time they vanished down the stairway to the Grotto, underneath me.

They were down there a long time, holding their service; I could hear their singing. The crowd around me, in the choir, was mainly of women and children, and in time the latter grew restless. They squirmed and fought and moved around. One boy shot off a cap pistol. Then eventually the *kawasses'* banging was heard again, and the procession came up the stairs. The white-gold river — candle-lit — flowed back, in the opposite direction, between its darker banks. And when the Custos himself came in sight he was carrying the Christ Child's effigy. But it was fully clad now, and seated on a golden throne, and the Custos held it high. As I watched it I could not but think of the Emerald Buddha in Thailand, which has its clothes changed to match the seasons. But I supposed the symbolism here had much more to it: Our Lord had finished His infancy and was going forth. The doll-like realism of the effigy was effective, too — the Arab women near me exclaimed with delight at it.

When the procession had passed, I left the church and went back to Jerusalem, for several hours of bathing, dining, and otherwise freshening up; and when I returned to Bethlehem, with friends, it was late in the evening. The church was lively, especially in the north transept, where the Copts and Syrians were both holding services — the Copts, like the Syrians, had begun much earlier, during the day, but I had missed them.

The Syrians had an altar in the transept's southeast corner, and the Copts had one in an apse, or semicircular bay, in its north. Each group included a few vested priests and a small lay following, and each was singing its own liturgy — the Copts in old Egyptian and the Syrians in Syriac or Aramaic. Meanwhile the Greeks, up in the choir, were singing *their* liturgy in Greek. The services were not a stone's throw apart, and their chanting struck the ears all together. "Is this how medieval polyphony developed?" I heard a voice say near me — it belonged to a young American I knew, from Jerusalem. It might be how it had developed at that, I mused — or perhaps how the Tower of Babel had. Yet oddly the three assorted groups, in their different tongues, were celebrating the self-same thing: the Gospel story of the Nativity.

I went out to the nave, and it was dark and shadowy up at the top now, among the wooden rafters. People were standing here and there, in knots, on the wide stone floor. When the knots were in the side aisles the columns there loomed high above them. The lighting of the place, because uneven — inefficient — was also dramatic and spectacular. The people moved about in it; and at the church's east end — above the choir — a wondrous glow could be seen now, of a chandelier and candles and all the icons.

I went back to the north transept, and the Copts were staging a small procession there. Then the Syrians staged one, too, all in the transept itself. They marched round, chanting, and waved their censers.

Back in the nave the crowd was thickening. The people there couldn't see or hear the Greek service well — it was up in the choir, by the icon screen, where places were hard to get. Instead they were standing round and waiting — waiting for a Greek procession that would start at midnight. They were restless, too. They were all life and movement, jostle and chat. The police were about among them — the spikes on their helmets could be seen above the sea of heads.

The procession, when it came, was a grand one. It had all the elegance and richness that the Greeks seemed so proficient in. It went round the nave three times — and up the middle at the end — and it filled the great space with its chants and candlelight. There were the boys in purple and the Patriarch and the vested priests; and among the notables who followed, also bearing candles, were the Anglican Archbishop and the tall Muhafez — the latter wearing tails, white tie, and many medals.

They went round and round the church slowly, singing the liturgy. Then eventually they went back to the choir, and for the crowd the evening was over. A policeman took the Muhafez out immediately, and a *kawass* took out the Anglican Archbishop. But the rest of us jammed up, for ages, at the little door.

The next day I took it easy, as on the Latin Christmas. I did go watch the line-crossers returning for a while, though. Many of them were laden down, as the policeman had predicted — one woman even had a basket so heavy that she couldn't carry it; she just hitched it along on the ground; and on top of it some coconuts and apples could be seen. There was much emotion, too, as the crossers left their relatives. People sobbed, and grown men wiped tears from their eyes, as they went back through the customs. Then they disappeared, beyond the newest partition in that much-parted Holy Land.

A JERUSALEM INTERLUDE

IN THE GAPS between the Christmases I lived on in Jerusalem, using my time for research — for reading, that is, and for talking with some of the Christian priests and scholars in the city. I was curious, especially, about the division of rights between the sects, which I had begun finding in the Holy Places; and also, of course, about the sects themselves, and how they had come to be separate.

One document I found was a calendar of the Christmases made up by the Muhafazah, or Military Governor's office, in Jerusalem. It was well printed and long — thirty-two pages, both in English and in Arabic — and it gave minute directions for the rituals in Bethlehem of the Roman, Greek, Syrian, Coptic, and Armenian Churches. The calendar must have cost a good deal — by Jordanian standards — in money and pains, yet I imagine it was worth every bit of this to the Jerusalem authorities, albeit they were predominantly Moslem themselves. Their task of assisting at the rituals — and, especially, of keeping order at them — might have been impossible unless all moves, by all parties, had been described in black and white beforehand.

In reading the calendar I discovered many small issues between the Churches that I had not noticed when watching the services themselves. I learned, for instance, that when the Syrians had held their Christmas Eve ceremony in the Grotto of the Nativity, their officiant had had to stand "on the bare floor, as mats, carpets, etc., are not allowed." But when the Copts had done the same thing, their officiant had stood "on the carpet placed by the Greek Orthodox facing the Altar of the Star." Since the freedom to place equipment in the Christian shrines — as I had been learning — is related to other, more permanent rights there, I took these notes as showing not only the low estate of the Syrians in the Grotto, but also the dependence of the Copts, for their slightly higher estate, on the tolerance of the Greeks.

Elsewhere the calendar specified just when the different sects' icons, candles, and other utensils should be put on, and taken off, the various altars; and these directions seemed to have almost the nature of international law. One of them, concerning candles, is worth quoting in full as a sample of the atmosphere prevailing. It comes from the rules for the Roman Catholic Epiphany procession, which at one stage uses the Altar of the Star of the Nativity in the Grotto, although Greek Christmas Eve services have been in progress there.

Immediately before this procession arrives at the Grotto of the Nativity [the direction says] the Government official in charge of the Christmas religious ceremonies requests the Orthodox representative present in the Grotto to extinguish the two Orthodox candles on the Altar of the Star. In case the Orthodox representative refrains from so doing the Government official in charge will direct the District Officer of the Bethlehem Sub-District to extinguish the two candles in question. Should the Orthodox representative protest against such an action a note of the protest should be taken by the Government official in charge and placed on Government official records.

To a seasoned Christmas-goer in the Holy Land this item means at least three things. First, the Catholics have established a right to use the altar at the time concerned. Second, the Greeks don't recognize this right, and are loath to do anything that might confirm it. And third, the action needed to harmonize the two positions can be taken only by a non-partisan authority, namely the Jordanian government. This government acts like an international police force in the Christmas festivities — one comes to feel when studying the matter — and the various Churches act not unlike hostile nations.

Some time after reading that calendar I came on another document, a memorandum about the so-called Status Quo in the Holy Places, written by a British civil servant in the nineteen twenties, when Britain, under the Palestine Mandate, was playing the international-police role herself — she had taken it over from the Turks, who had previously held it for four centuries. According to the memorandum, the Status Quo was a legal code — the writer placed it among "the most fluid and imprecise" ones in the world — that the Turkish Sultan had enunciated in the mid-nineteenth century. For a couple of centuries before that, apparently, the dominant role in the Holy Places had shifted back and forth between the Catholics and the Greeks, depending on which had bribed the Turks more liberally — the Turks themselves had made vast sums out of the rivalry, I gathered as I read, and meanwhile the smaller Churches had been greatly reduced in their rights because their purses had been limited. But by the mid-nineteenth century this Turkish leeway to make bargains had become a liability, not an asset, for the Holy Places were by then deeply involved in European power politics. The Status Quo was accordingly declared, and — however "fluid and imprecise" — it lasted as long as the Turkish rule did. And thereafter the British themselves used it, during the Mandate — which began in 1920 — as the basis of their administration of the Holy Places (the memorandum that I saw had been written as a guide in this).

The Status Quo did not concern the Christian Holy Places alone, I learned on reading about it. It applied also to the Wailing Wall in Jerusalem — a scene of hot conflict between Arabs and Jews under the Mandate — as well as to Rachel's Tomb, in Bethlehem's outskirts, where the rivalry had been likewise between Arabs and Jews. (Indeed there must have been some rivalry over Rachel's Tomb among the Jews themselves, for I read that both the main Jewish communities, the Sephardim and the Ashkenazim, had held keys to the shrine — keys being a leading symbol of rights. But I found no suggestion in the memorandum of violence, like that of the Christian sects, between the two.)

The Status Quo was a declaration of still-pond-no-more-moving that, as enforced by the British in the 'twenties — and also, I gathered, by the Jordanians at present — greatly hindered repairs to the Church of the Nativity and other Holy Places. Under it no such work could be done without permission from all the sects concerned, for the sect that paid the bill might thereby strengthen its claim on the shrine improved. In the memorandum I found confirmation, for instance, of what an Armenian priest had told me: that his people could not alter their dark and primitive

monastery adjoining the Church of the Nativity because
certain of the other sects, who had dormant claims there,
would not allow the Armenian rights to be thus reinforced.
I also read that in 1926 the roof on the Church of the
Nativity had needed repairs badly; that the Catholics and
the Armenians had demanded to share in paying for them;
but that the Greeks, whose rights were dominant there,
had refused this and had thereby hung the project up. I
read about many other things, too: about how the Catholics, for instance, had established the right after many incidents, more or less violent, to clean the narrow strip of
floor by which they passed, through territory normally
Armenian, between their own church and the Grotto of
the Nativity — the right to clean a Holy Place being con-
struable, like the right to repair one, as partial grounds for
control.

 Meanwhile, in between my reading, I was walking
around Jerusalem. One place I often visited was the Church
of the Holy Sepulchre, a Christian shrine roughly equal
to the Church of the Nativity in age and importance and
in the warmth of its inter-sect struggles (the keys to it
were held not by Christians, but by hereditary Moslem
caretakers whose forebears had been appointed in 636 by
the Caliph Omar — he thinking this was the only way to
ensure peace between the Christian sects there). Inside the
church I saw that great scaffoldings had been erected and
that repairs either had begun or were soon contemplated.
And I also heard that the Greek Orthodox Church had re-
sisted these repairs, out of fear that they might uncover
ancient Crusader work and thus strengthen the Roman
Catholic position in the place. So I looked up a scholarly
Protestant I knew and asked him about the matter.

"Yes," he answered, "it is much as you have heard it.

In the early eighteenth century the Greeks renovated the
Church of the Holy Sepulchre — they had a strong hand
in Jerusalem then — and they are accused of having covered up as many Crusader touches as they could. They
are now said to be hanging back from new renovations
because they don't want these features to be revealed. But
the Greeks say, in effect, 'Why stress the Crusaders anyway? They are a bad memory — a memory of violence.'
The Arabs, as you may know, liken the Crusader kingdom
to Israel — they describe both as Western attempts to
create a religious state in Palestine by force. So the Greeks
say 'Let's stress not the Crusader churches, but our own
Orthodox ones, which were here even before Islam came.'
Before the Crusades, it is believed, the Christian population in the Holy Land was more or less equal to the Islamic,
but after the Crusades it diminished greatly. And the Crusaders pressed the Greeks a lot, too, wanting them to recognize the Pope's supremacy and things like that. All this
background makes for a bad feeling that still exists. Also
the Catholics are proselytizing among the Orthodox congregation in the Holy Land, and that makes for jealousy.
And when there is a question of repairs to a church, the
Catholics are rich and can urge that it be done on a big
scale, whereas the Greeks hold back because they can't
pay much themselves and don't want the Catholics paying
a lot and thereby gaining status. The Catholics maintain
that they are a big, important body, of course, and deserve
better rights in, say, the Church of the Nativity. To which
the Greeks reply, 'Well, the Catholics have good times of
day, anyway, for their services in these churches.' But actually the Greeks have much the best of it in regard to places.''

This statement proved largely unassailable as my researches went on, though the Catholics and Israelis might

have denied some parts of it. A Catholic priest was later to criticize, in conversation with me, the *Protestant,* not the Latin, proselytizing among the Orthodox. And most Israelis would perhaps have laughed at the Arab objection to creating religious states by force in Palestine, as that is what the Arabs had done themselves. In fact the mixing of religion, force, and politics — quite beyond separability — seemed endemic there.*

The long Christmas season was cozy in Jerusalem. There was much visiting back and forth — along with drinking of tea, coffee, wine, brandy, and other solvents — by the different priesthoods and the officialdom. There was also bright, sunny weather every day. This last was a mixed blessing — as it meant the continuance of the drought — yet at least it was an unfailing topic of conversation, and also of prayer. People meeting in the Old City's narrow streets would talk about the drought; and right after our Western — Gregorian — New Year's Day a Franciscan father, whom I bumped into, informed me that his order had begun praying systematically for rain. The next day the sky was gray for a while, indeed, but nothing fell from it; and before long the Greeks got more of a feather in their cap, climatically speaking, than the Latins; for early on their Christmas morning it showered heavily. The south wind blew then and the rain came down in buckets, and the Greek liturgy was widely, if but half seriously, given credit for this. Yet the shower lasted only a few hours in the end, and the water ran off the stone-hard ground immediately, so that little was accomplished. The dry weather continued, and I walked around in the sun.

* The mixture had a long history before Christian or Islamic times, too — a history running through the careers of Joshua, David, Samson, and the Maccabees, to name only a few of the protagonists.

On the Julian New Year's Day — our January fourteenth
— the Greek Church had a cake-cutting, which I attended.
The room where it occurred was warm with rugs and a
stove, and it also held a throne and rows of folding chairs.
I sat well back in these, while at the front were notables,
among them Jerusalem's extremely tall Muhafez. Many
local people were seated around me, all dressed up, and
others were standing packed together in the rear — they
were the cream, I gathered, of the city's Orthodox community. Essentially the scene was like an American Christ-
mas-tree affair, but staged more richly — vested priests and
choir-boys, for instance, sang in Greek. The cake was in
a shallow Arab pan a yard in diameter; and the small,
bearded, vigorous-looking Greek Patriarch made the first
few cuts in it. He slashed away with a long knife while a
pretty little girl, dressed in white — even a white overcoat
— assisted him. But soon he handed the knife to a layman
carver. The cake, when I got some, was sweet and spicy,
though whether Greek or Arabic in style I do not know. It
was handed out with wrapping paper, and soon I put most
of mine in my pocket and said good-bye; for the gathering,
though warm and friendly, was not really for outsiders.

I can't define that room's function in the Patriarchate,
or even its physical position there, as the whole place was
a labyrinth I never figured out. Part of it was built into
the complex of the Holy Sepulchre itself, in Jerusalem's
heart. Then from there it extended westward — crossing
at least one street by terraces overhead, atop stone arches
— till finally it spread out into myriad small courts and
buildings. I penetrated to a few of these courtyards during
my stay, and they were always pleasant — with flagstones,
whitewashed walls, blue-painted woodwork, and green
things growing on the window-sills (if only from tin cans

there). Everything showed the feeling for beauty that I had been noting in the Greeks.

The Catholic establishment seemed less poetic — less other-worldly — in appearance, though it too was archaic by Western standards. Actually there were two establishments, so far as I was concerned: the Patriarchate itself — which I had visited on December twenty-fourth — and Saint Savior's monastery, where dwelt most of the Franciscan monks who served in the Holy Places. Like the Patriarchate, Saint Savior's was made of tawny limestone and was also built against the Old City's western wall. It was a huge place, like some community of the Middle Ages. It housed, among other things, a big church, a big school, and a printing press that had turned out many books. The priests living there were numbered in the hundreds, I think — at least they were enough to be an ever-recurring sight as they walked, in their brown robes, through the city. I came to know Franciscans of various nationalities — including, especially, Americans and Belgians — but the great majority were Italians; and Italian was the tongue they spoke in common. (Their order had charge of the Holy Places because Saint Francis had come to Palestine during the Crusades, and he had believed in dramatizing the faith by shrines and pageantry.)

Early in that season I visited the Syrians' headquarters, for I wished to talk with the young priest there whom I had met in Bethlehem — I shall call him Brother John. I found him in his room or cell, which was typical of many Eastern priests' living quarters in Jerusalem. Its rough stone walls were whitewashed and very thick — its single window was set in a recess several feet deep. Its wooden door was but loosely fitted in its frame, and the whole place was chilly and austere. Clothes hung from pegs in the wall, and books and other things lay on open shelves. There were also three or four inexpensive, bright-colored religious pictures in evidence.

Brother John welcomed me effusively and began by showing me around the monastery, which was called Saint Mark's — it was a small place, but a fascinating specimen, even by Holy Land standards, of ancient limestone architecture. It was on the "traditional" site of a meeting-place of Christ and the apostles — the Last Supper had occurred there, traditionally, and so had Christ's appearance to Saint Thomas, after His Resurrection, and the Holy Ghost's descent at Pentecost. Brother John told me of all this as he showed me around; and along the way we met a couple of older Syrian priests whom I had likewise seen at Bethlehem — they had a tough, rather Biblical look, with weatherbeaten faces and grizzled beards. (In theory a metropolitan or bishop resides at Saint Mark's, but he was not there now and we did not mention him, for he was in fact *persona non grata* in Jordan, having removed some of the Dead Sea scrolls from the country a few years earlier. I think he was living in New Jersey at the time of my visit.)

After our tour we went back to Brother John's room, where he sat me down, offered me candy from a tin box and began to talk. He was a thin young man, emotional and intense. He had a clear skin illumined, it seemed, by a flush underneath it, and his long dark beard came up high on his cheeks. His hair was long, too, and on it he wore the knitted black cap of the Syrian priests — or especially of the celibate ones, as I learned from him. He talked quickly, fluently, enthusiastically, and with ill-disguised partisanship — he gave the impression that nearly all the world's strength, courage, and brilliance were concentrated in the Syrian fold. He made old history sound interesting, too, if somewhat like a series of wild rumors.

He began by telling of the earliest times. "The first Christians in the Holy Land were Jews by origin," he said. "But they had to leave here when Titus crushed Jerusalem in 70 A.D. They went away to Pella, over beyond the Jordan, and that was the end of them — they couldn't come back even in the second century, because Hadrian renewed the anti-Jewish policy of Titus, and so their Church died out in exile. But meanwhile the Syrian Christians had come here from the north, and from Mesopotamia, and they kept the faith in the Holy Land alive. Their language was Syriac or Aramaic, you know — the language used by Christ — and they were under the Patriarch of Antioch. He was the first Patriarch of all — Saint Peter had ordained him before going to Rome." *

These Syriac or Syrian Christians, according to Brother John, had built the first church of Saint Mark's — on the site where we were talking — in 73 A.D., and for more than two hundred years thereafter the Christians in the Holy Land had been Syriac almost exclusively. They had been persecuted off and on by their Roman overlords, but when Constantine had made Christianity the state religion, early in the fourth century, life had grown easier for them. Brother John even told me that Saint Helena, Constantine's mother, had been the daughter of a Syrian married priest, but I did not find this borne out by other sources.

* More detached historians point out that Syriac or Aramaic was spoken throughout the Holy Land in the first century — it was spoken by virtually all of Christendom then, not by a small fraction thereof as at present. So there is scant reason to believe in a movement of Syriac-speaking Christians "down from the north," though this belief is strong with modern Syrian Christians, who do represent that smaller region (North Syria and Northwest Mesopotamia).

Anyway harmony had prevailed, in the newly Christian world, till about 430, when the so-called Nestorian Heresy had arisen to split the eastern part of the Syrian Church away from the western part, and also from the Christians in Europe. Brother John did not explain the theory of this Nestorian controversy — and I despaired of getting him to — but he did make it plain that he had a low opinion of the whole affair; he described it as a trick used by the Europeans against the Asiatics. "The Byzantines and Latins put divisions in the great Syrian Church," he said, "because there is a saying that if you divide a people you can govern them all."

Nor did he think any more of another issue, the so-called Monophysite Heresy, which had come along two decades later and had split the remaining Syrians — plus the Armenians, Copts, and Ethiopians — away from Europe. Again he did not explain the controversy, but he conveyed a great sense of regional fervor about it.

"In the fourth century," he said, "we had three thousand monasteries and ninety thousand monks around Edessa in Syria alone. But then the Greeks began slaying us as Monophysites. They slew and slew. They slew us in our monasteries. Millions of us." This figure was a slip, perhaps — at least it was an exaggeration. But there was no questioning it, for Brother John was worked up now, sitting forward and with eyes alight. He showed me a high-sign used by the Monophysites in those old days — it involved the thumb and first two fingers, especially the index finger. "Because of this sign," he said, "the Greeks cut off our index fingers when they were persecuting us. They cut off forty camel-loads of fingers, altogether, and carried them away — and a camel, you know, can take three hundred kilograms."

I didn't question this statistic, either, but encouraged him to go on. "That is why the Greek priests wear their hair long now," he said; "from sadness for the massacres. And we Syrians did not forgive them. Because of our hatred we helped the Moslem Arabs conquer all this region from the Byzantines in the seventh century. And until the tenth century the Arabs were very sweet to us. We call it the golden time. And we gave them all their education." But then the relationship had gone sour, and the Arabs and other Moslems had persecuted the Syrian Christians, intermittently, ever since. "As late as 1914," Brother John said, "the Moslem Kurds bombarded Syrian Christians up north of here with artillery — but the cannonballs bounced back, miraculously, at them.

"The Turks massacred us several times," he continued. "They hung our bishops over the doorways, like cats. Two hundred and seventy-five years ago they massacred fifteen thousand of us here in Jerusalem. Before that we had six monasteries here and many rights in the Holy Places. Then afterward our brothers the Armenians took care of those rights. We would do it for them, too. It is the custom — if one is massacred, the other one takes care. But the Armenians were just like Judas. We had only an old monk here with one eye, and an old archbishop came to join him. The Armenians would say, 'You are old, and sweeping is hard; let us do it for you,' or they would say, 'You cannot see those candles well; let us light them for you.' And the old archbishop let them — in his innocence — and now they hold those places. They hold them as servants of the Syrians, but they hold them. And they bribed the Turks, too. You know that altar in the Church of the Nativity where I saw you at Christmas. That is our altar really. But the Armenians bribed the Turks and put their

icon there, and now they hold it." Then Brother John returned to the Moslems, and their persecution of the Syrians, and he talked a good while longer.

After that I wanted some better information on the
Nestorians and Monophysites. I chanced, as a matter of
fact, to know something about Nestorian Christians already, for I had come on reports of them farther east in
Asia. They had been the great Christian missionaries in
that continent in the first millennium A.D., and their scope
there had been almost as great as that of the Western missionaries — Catholic and Protestant — in modern times. I
had read that they had established churches all the way
across Central Asia, as far as Peking; and when living in
China in the nineteen forties I had met an old Englishman
who collected Nestorian crosses, of a peculiar shape, that
he said were found on the edge of the Gobi Desert. Later
on, in India, I had become aware of a big community of
so-called Syrian Christians on the Malabar Coast, and I
believe these were Nestorians, too — the faith having per-
sisted there while it was wiped out in China and Central
Asia.

While knowing of the great dispersion of that Church,
though, I still was unfamiliar with its doctrines, and I
began looking them up. I read somewhat — Jerusalem being well endowed with literature on such things — and I
also went to two young American Catholic priests I knew,
who were studying in the city; I shall call them Fathers
Smith and Collins. Besides being intelligent they were well
trained in the Western way of looking at things — scholarly, precise, and unemotional — though of course if there
were two sides to a question, the Catholic and another,
they would take the Catholic.

They told me a lot about the early Church, which I shan't go into here. Disputes flourished in it, but they did not turn into heresies with big labels until theology was organized by Constantine, who wanted a centralized religion to go with his centralized empire.* In 325 A.D. he called the Ecumenical Council of Nicea (ecumenical, as applied to the Church, meaning universal), which adopted the Nicene Creed — still used throughout Christendom — and condemned the Arian Heresy. (The latter lived on for some time among the Germanic tribes, but finally died out without establishing a church.)

The Nicene Creed said that Christ was "of one substance with the Father," to quote the English translation, but this did not end all argument on the subject. In the next century various lesser heresies sprang up, with names like Sabellianism, Tritheism, and Semi-Arianism. Then along came Nestorianism — named for Nestorius, a Syrian priest — which held that Christ had actually been two distinct persons, one human and one divine. This idea was inspired mainly, so far as I could learn, by the problem of the Virgin Mary's nature: the Nestorians held that Mary had been mortal and could not have given birth to a god — rather, they said, she had produced a human with whom divinity had later been associated.

The Fathers told me that Nestorianism was condemned by the Ecumenical Council of Ephesus, in 431, which decided that there was only one person in Christ and also

---

* Since reading this account in *The New Yorker*, Father Collins has supplied me with certain comments and corrections. Of this passage he writes: "Constantine was seeking not to establish but to preserve an already well-established religion, which was then being threatened by the prospect of disunity, due to the heresy of Arianism. (This heresy taught that the Son was not truly divine, but a creature. Hence, Nicea stressed the 'consubstantiality' of the Son with the Father.)"

that the Virgin should be called *Theotokos,* or God-bearer. After that the Nestorians split off from Antioch and based themselves in Mesopotamia — they became a schismatic, farther-eastern Church on their own. Then two decades later Monophysitism arose. Apparently it was the exact opposite of Nestorianism — and a reaction to it — for it held that Christ had not only been one person, but had had one "nature" or *physis* too, the divine in Him having sublimated, or transformed, the human.*

"Monophysitism began in Alexandria," Father Collins said. "And then it spread throughout the Church in Asia. It attracted many pious elements who wanted to regard Our Lord's divinity, rather than his humanity. But it was condemned by the Council of Chalcedon, in 451, which agreed that Our Lord, while only one person, had had both a divine and a human nature. After that Monophysitism didn't die, though, but continued underground in the Eastern congregations. By 500 it was very strong in Alexandria, and the situation in Asia — in Armenia, Syria, and Palestine — was chaotic, too."

"It was Greek monks who saved Jerusalem from going Monophysite," said Father Smith. "They moved down here from Cappadocia, in Asia Minor, and they infiltrated the local Church. It was quite a struggle, but they won out in the end, and that is why the Greek Orthodox are so strong in the Holy Land today. But the Syriac-speaking Church went Monophysite itself. So did the Armenian, Coptic, and Ethiopian Churches — and that is why they are separate now, of course."

---

* The questions touched on so briefly here have occupied years in the lives of eminent theologians, who even then could not agree on them. Readers wishing to pursue the subject might look up the different heresies in the Encyclopedia Britannica, which in turn will give further references.

At that point I asked the natural foolish question of a layman: What difference had these issues made to those involved? "Pragmatically," I said, "could it have mattered to a worshipper whether he believed that Our Lord had had one or two persons, or one or two natures?"

"Oh, in those days," said Father Smith, "people could never have looked at it pragmatically. They didn't think that way." *

"Besides," said Father Collins, "if Nestorius was right, then only part of Our Lord died on the cross. And if Monophysitism was right, on the other hand, there was no human suffering involved."

He stopped then as if all questions had been answered, and I suppose they had, if one held the Catholic beliefs about Christ's sacrifice. But to go outside these for a moment, I would note a few other considerations that I think applied.

For one thing, Greek philosophy was rife throughout all Christendom in those early centuries, having come down through the Hellenistic and Roman periods substantially

---

* "This may be an accurate quote of one of us," writes Father Collins, "but I believe it is misleading, especially in the context of your question: 'could it have mattered to a worshipper . . . ?' I think your question situates the problem precisely where it did most matter: to a worshipper. This would be obvious against the Arian background: if Jesus Christ is only a creature, even though the greatest, it would be unthinkable to worship him as God. To a Nestorian, the object of his worship is the divine person, to whom the human Jesus is connected by a close union, but the person being worshipped is *not* the man who lived and died. And in the worship of a Monophysite (from the point of view, again, of Orthodox criticism), there is a surrendering of the basic Christian mystery that this person being worshipped as truly divine is at the same time truly human, truly 'one of us' in all things save sin. Another way of putting all this: from the Orthodox point of view, the basic Christian reality of the Redemption is vitiated by both the Monophysite and the Nestorian views (to say nothing of the Arian!)."

intact. It had established schools in all the civilized towns, and no creed, apparently, could get around it — or around its insistence that everything, including the unknowable, should be scrutinized by logic.

Then there must also have been a widespread fear, in the Church, that Christianity would slip back into the old paganism, or into some new heresy like Arianism; and against that risk the best safeguard must have seemed to be a careful definition of the Trinity, and especially of Christ.

Finally there had been the old, old struggle of Asia against Europe. Sitting in the Holy Land now, I did not find it hard to see the Byzantines using their Church as a harness for the Asians and the Africans. And I could see the latter contending against this, and trying to slip away — without giving up their faith essentially — by means of doctrinal disputes.

I also learned something, in my Christmas pauses, about the schism between the Greeks and Latins, which came much later than the early heresies. Doctrinally this mainly hinged, as I understand it, on the world *Filioque*. The Nicene Creed said that the Holy Ghost "proceedeth from the Father," but in the eighth century the Latin Church — partly through ancient fear, it is said, of Arianism among the Goths — inserted *Filioque* ("and from the Son") at the end of this phrase. The Byzantines never forgave that re-arrangement — not so much because they disliked it for itself, apparently, as because they couldn't tolerate a purely Roman change in a creed adopted by the full Church.*

* As time went on, though, the Byzantines did begin attacking the *Filioque* on grounds of dogma.

There were other ritualistic differences, too — the Greeks were using leavened bread and watered wine in their communion, for one thing, while the Latins were not. But again regional or political issues seem to have been very important — the great underlying one being the Pope's growing power, of which the Greeks were wary; and the immediate, precipitating one being the Crusades. The Crusaders, though coming eastward ostensibly to help the Byzantine Church against the Arabs, actually treated that Church roughly. They sacked Constantinople once; they deposed Eastern prelates; and they made converts among the Eastern flocks. They were often headstrong and barbaric, and on entering Jerusalem they massacred the Arabs there wholesale, thus making a return to co-existence in the Holy City — which was vital to the Greeks — more difficult than ever.

As for the Pope, his development was very different from that of the Patriarch in Constantinople. The latter was merely a religious leader subject to the Byzantine emperor; he had a sophisticated laity, by and large, with the tradition of Greek philosophy behind it; and for these reasons he did not become an autocrat, either temporal or ideological. The Pope, on the other hand, had the no-nonsense Roman tradition of law and organization behind him; he functioned in a political chaos, rather than an empire, and with a mainly illiterate laity; and so he and his hierarchy became the great authority in their world.

As the Roman system got more and more tightly organized, of course, the Greeks found it harder and harder to accept Rome's claim to leadership. Meanwhile the two Churches, with their different languages, were drifting apart inevitably because of bad medieval communications; there was a series of misunderstandings and incidents, leading to virtual schism in the eleventh century; and then after 1453 — when the Turks seized Constantinople and put the Orthodox behind their curtain — the break was complete.

I got much of this analysis from sources other than Fathers Smith and Collins, needless to say, but the Fathers did tell me a lot about Rome's more recent connections with the East. To a large extent these involve the so-called Uniat churches, which have been coming into existence since the Crusades.

"Uniat congregations," said Father Smith, "are Eastern ones that have returned to the Church under Rome, but have not given up their old liturgies and customs. In effect Uniat means Catholic, and a better term for Uniat Christians is 'Greek-Rite Catholics,' or 'Syrian-Rite Catholics,' or whatever they may be. One of the biggest and oldest Uniat churches is the Maronite. The Maronites broke off from the Syrian Church long, long ago, and then during the Crusades they were admitted to the Roman Church. Their head is called the 'Maronite Patriarch of Antioch and all the East,' but actually the church is a Lebanese affair. The president of Lebanon must be a Maronite, you know, while the prime minister must be a Moslem. There are a good many Maronites in America, too."

Indeed most of the Uniat churches are represented in America, the Fathers told me, and that is why one hears so often of Eastern-Rite Catholics there. Apart from the Maronites, who came over *in toto,* the Uniat churches have all been detached from existing Eastern Churches, so that each of them has a schismatic parallel, as the Fathers put it. For instance the Syrian-Rite Catholic Church was detached from the Syrian Monophysites. And there is also an *East* Syrian Uniat church — more usually called the

Chaldean Church — which was detached from the Nestorians. It is under the Patriarch of Babylon in Mosul, Syria.

"There are many Armenian Catholics, too," said Father Smith, "and their patriarch is Cardinal Agagianian, who, as you may remember, has been talked of as a possible Pope. There is a Coptic Uniat Church, and also a large Ethiopian one — especially in Italian Somaliland, where the Jesuits have made much progress lately. When a Uniat church is established in America it is apt to Latinize its liturgy a good deal — so as to be more like the majority of Catholics there — but the Church discourages this on the whole. Another problem arises in America because of the Eastern married priests. Many Eastern priests are married, and this holds true for the Uniat churches like the rest. So Uniat married priests often go and serve in America, and the Latin Catholics there are sometimes shocked when they learn about them."

I never did run down, even with the Fathers' help, a total list of the Eastern Churches that have distinctive names. The question is complicated, anyway, by the fact that some Churches go under special names in certain regions — the Syrian Monophysite Church, for instance, is known in America variously as the Syrian Church of Antioch and the *As*syrian Church of Antioch.

Nor did I try to list all the patriarchs in existence, except for the Roman Catholic and Greek Orthodox ones, whom I have already mentioned. I think there are a great many, both patriarchs and Churches — the latter being represented quite fully, as a matter of fact, in places like New Jersey and industrial Connecticut.

Father Collins told me a little about Pope John XXIII's effort to bring the Churches together again. "Pope John

was the papal nuncio in Istanbul for some time," he said,
"and while there he developed a great sympathy for the
Greek Orthodox. He is now trying to call an Ecumenical
Council — he has sent out feelers to the Greeks and the
Protestants about it. Of course there are great problems in
the way. The Eastern Churches have changed very little
over the centuries, whereas the Western has changed a lot
— what with the Reformation, the Counter-Reformation,
the growth of modern science, the opening of the New
World, and all that. The Western Church has become
much more organized than the others. If the others came
back they might not have to accept all this — they might
stay out of the organization somewhat. It wouldn't be easy,
but at least a few people are thinking along that line."

Some time after our conversation — in 1962 — Pope
John's Ecumenical Council was indeed called, in Rome,
but the Greeks were not there. A main reason for their
absence, one gathers, has been the abiding Eastern fear of
Latin strength. And that fear was expressed to me by another priest in my Jerusalem holiday season — an Armenian whom I shall call Father Turusian. "The Latin
Church is a big fish," he told me, "and we others are little
fishes. Big fishes like to swallow little ones, and our job is
not to let that happen."

Father Turusian was perhaps the most enjoyable of all
my Christmas acquaintances in Jerusalem. He was a strong
and square-built man, though small. He had a well-shaped
head and small square hands; and his beard, also small,
was black and white. He was always cheerful and humorous
when I saw him, and I think this was his unfailing attitude.
He told me he had spent some years in America — as, in
fact, had several other Armenian priests in Jerusalem. He
had had two parishes in Massachusetts mill towns, another

in New Jersey, and another in Canada; and he had also been on a Church-diplomatic mission to Iran, where there is a sizable Armenian community.

He explained that the Armenians had a "diaspora," somewhat like the Jewish one, and that this fact had much influence on their Church. Their hierarchy had a traditional center, he said, at Etchmiadzin, near Erivan, in what is now Soviet Armenia; and a prelate held sway there who was widely recognized as "Supreme Catholicos of all Armenians." But the Cold War had lessened his hold on his flock, and there was a movement against him in the diaspora. The Armenian Church in Jerusalem had been involved in this struggle, as a matter of fact, and so had Father Turusian himself, though I was not to learn much about it until later.

The Armenian diaspora is spread over most of the world, I gathered, but a sizable part of it lives right in Jerusalem. The nucleus of this community goes far back in time, but the bulk of it came only four decades ago, as a result of the big Turkish massacres of Armenians. The refugees came down to Jerusalem, and many of them lodged in the Armenian monastery there, which is called Saint James'. Many have lodged in it ever since, and one or two thousand were said to be there at the time of my visit — men, women, and children packed into the place as if still on an emergency basis.

Father Turusian was living there, too, and he received me in his room — it was the usual small, bare, white-washed cell. He offered me candy from the usual tin box and told me a good deal about his Church's history, though I shan't repeat much of it here. The Armenians accepted Christianity fairly early, it seems — their king made it the state religion in A.D. 303, thus founding the first state

Church in Christendom. It has differed from most of the other Churches in that it hasn't proselytized much — if at all — outside its own nationality, and it has therefore run close to the national life and played an intimate part in it. Indeed the Armenian Church seems, as one hears its history, to be an especially durable and close-knit island of Christendom, though far away from the rest — well out in Asia — and cut off, through the centuries, by hostile territory.

"We think there have been Armenian Christians in Jerusalem from very early times," Father Turusian said. "The Romans had an Armenian legion in Asia Minor, and we think some of the soldiers came down here and were Christians. Later our first bishop, Saint Gregory the Illuminator, came to the Holy Land on a pilgrimage. And there was an Armenian patriarch here at least by the eighth century, for the Caliph recognized him then. But our strongest period was the Crusades. We controlled the Kingdom of Cilicia at that time. It was in Asia Minor, on the road from Europe to the Holy Land, and we were able to help both the Crusaders and the Greeks. Armenians fought alongside the Crusaders, and served as guides and interpreters for them, because we knew the Middle East much better than they did. So our position was strong. It is believed that we had big monasteries then in Palestine, and even whole villages. Old mosaics are often uncovered here now with Armenian writing on them. If the Catholics or Greeks uncover them, however, they sometimes cover them up again. At crucial times and places in the Holy Land, you see, there is apt to be a rivalry between the Catholics, the Greeks, and ourselves. The Syrians, Copts, and Ethiopians are apt to follow the Armenian lead in these matters, rather than contending on their own."

I doubt if Brother John, my Syrian acquaintance, would have endorsed this last statement, but I believe it gave the Armenian view in all good nature. Father Turusian was candid and humorous, too, in discussing other aspects of the Churches' strife. "I suppose an outsider must have trouble understanding it," he said. "But if you are taking part in the struggle yourself, and doing it to worship God, there is much more reason to it. Your struggling and your vigilance are tokens of your faith, and you must see that no one else outdoes you."

He told me more about the struggle's rules. "If you say a service or perform a ritual at a certain time," he said, "you have to keep on doing it. If you lapse two or three years, and then start again, there will be objections. And the cleaning of the Holy Places is important. The Latins are entitled to clean the outside of the Church of the Nativity, or certain parts of it. While doing so they always try to get in the windows and clean the inside, too. The Greeks fight them off, so the Latins cannot claim to own the place. And so each tests the other's diligence."

The Father gave me more details as well, but they did not change the picture I had formed; they only strengthened it. Then in time I rose to leave. He rose, too, for he had an errand in the city; and he got ready to go out. On his bare head he put a conical hat of stiff material — but capable of folding, as he showed me, for ease in traveling. Then over it he put his black Ku-Kluxish hood or cowl. It was smart, with its heavy watered silk, and it made him look impressive and a bit mysterious — not mundane — almost like a character from science fiction. "In Jerusalem," he said, "we are supposed to dress like this when going on the street. But I never used to do it in New Jersey. It might have caused a riot, don't you think?"

I said I did — and truthfully — and then we left.

The Copts and Ethiopians, too, have places in Jerusalem, and I visited them and learned something of those Churches. The two are connected, but in a puzzling, ambiguous way that seems very Eastern. The Coptic Church is an Egyptian affair — "Copt" and "Egypt" are the same word, originally, but distorted differently by time. Traditionally — so Fathers Smith and Collins told me — the Coptic Church was founded by Saint Mark the Evangelist, who went to Alexandria, probably from Rome, in the first century A.D. Alexandria had been a great center of Greek culture, in both the Hellenistic and Roman periods, and so the Coptic Church — or rather, at that stage, the see of the Alexandrine Patriarch — played a big role in early Christendom. But later the Monophysite struggle cut it off from the European Churches, and then in the seventh century Islam conquered Egypt, after which the Christians there lingered on as a minority.

The origins of the Ethiopian Church are more obscure. One fact about it seems clear, though: it was *not* founded by the eunuch of Candace, the Ethiopian Queen, whom Saint Philip baptized soon after Christ's death, according to the Acts of the Apostles. Nothing more was heard of that missionary effort, apparently, and the faith was not lastingly implanted in Ethiopia, so far as is known, until the fourth century.

"Early in that century," Father Collins told me, "a certain Theophilus of India — actually a native of Ceylon, and an Arian — tried to convert the Ethiopians. But the conversions that really took hold, it is believed, were made right after that by a boy from Tyre. He was presumably a Syrian Christian, but the Church he founded was put under

Athanasius, the Patriarch of Alexandria. Then later, about 500 A.D., nine monks with Syrian names are said to have appeared in Ethiopia. They brought the Monophysite influence with them, but they did not detach the Ethiopian Church from the Coptic."

Father Smith added that the Ethiopian liturgy is fundamentally a Coptic one (that of Saint Cyril), and also that the Ethiopian Church is governed by a metropolitan, or bishop, who in turn is customarily ordained by the Patriarch of Alexandria. I got the impression, however, that the relationship is less simple than this sounds. I had trouble in talking with Ethiopian priests in the Holy Land, because of the language barrier, but they did seem clearly opposed to the suggestion that they were one with the Copts.

I imagine that the secular relations between Egypt and Ethiopia had much to do with this division. At that moment Gamal Abdel Nasser was leaning heavily toward Russia, while Haile Selassie was leaning toward the West. In the circumstances it would be natural for the Ethiopians to fight shy of the Copts, for fear of infiltration, and I suppose they were doing so.* I suppose, too, that they had often done so in the past for similar reasons. And then there was the distance — nearly two thousand miles — between Alexandria and Addis Ababa, not to mention the gulf between the two languages and cultures. The relationship seemed made for schisms.

Concerning the rights of those two Churches in the Holy Places, I found some information in the memorandum on

* It was around the end of the Second World War, I have been told, that Haile Selassie got the Alexandrine Patriarch to consecrate Ethiopian bishops in the Ethiopian Church — before that they had been Copts. So the fundamental change antedated Nasser by some years.

the Status Quo, which I have mentioned. Both Churches were almost squeezed out in the seventeenth century, apparently, by the high cost of Turkish bribes, but the Copts made a comeback in the nineteenth. Early in that century a military leader, Mohammed Ali, arose to make Egypt almost independent of the Turkish Empire, to which it theoretically belonged; and as his power grew he sent an army under his son, Ibrahim Pasha, way up to Syria, in a defense-through-offense move. Ibrahim occupied the Holy Land for a decade or two, and in this time Coptic priests and laymen moved there in good number — finding themselves in a privileged position, naturally enough, compared with other Christians.* Then in 1838, by chance, a plague attacked Jerusalem, and all the Ethiopian priests there died. Whereupon — according to the memorandum — the Copts persuaded Ibrahim Pasha to let them burn the Ethiopians' documents, including their title-deeds, on the grounds that they were all infected.

Whether this ruse actually kept the Ethiopians from returning to their property — and if so for how long — I did not learn; but later in the nineteenth century, at any rate, they found a defender in Czarist Russia, who was seeking ways to throw her weight around in the Middle East. She fixed on the Ethiopians' cause as one such way, and apparently was effective in it. At least the Ethiopians again held rights in Jerusalem by the time of the Mandate, when the memorandum was written. The rights were in dispute then, though, and the British evidently heard much argument about them. The Ethiopians were naturally unable to produce their deeds, burned so long ago. They maintained, however, that these still existed, though in

* I am told that the Copts had enjoyed a previous good period in the Holy Land when backed by the Mameluke rulers of Egypt.

Ethiopia and somewhat out of reach. At one point they claimed that they were in the hands of an elusive Russian baron there — his name, they said, was Nicholas Chef d'Oeuvre.

The fantastic improbability of all this was not lost on the Mandatory authorities, but still the Ethiopians held on. When I was in Jerusalem they had a reasonably good position there (though not in Bethlehem), and so did the Copts. The latter had a biggish compound right near the Church of the Holy Sepulchre, with a church of its own, a school, and some fifteen resident monks — besides holding services in the Holy Places these ministered to a Coptic flock in the Holy Land, left over from Ibrahim Pasha's time, which they said numbered three thousand. They also had a little Coptic shrine, right next to the Sepulchre itself, which they looked on as a prize possession. (The décor of their monastery seemed rather lush, out of keeping with the city's limestone crudeness. And the monks themselves seemed a bit dispirited, perhaps because of conditions in their homeland — the Coptic Church had been having a hard time, I think, with Nasser's Moslem nationalism.)

As for the Ethiopians, they had a monastery that was near the heart of things, being built on the roof of an old church, held by the Armenians, which adjoins the Church of the Holy Sepulchre and supposedly dates from Saint Helena's time. This church's roof is flat, and the Ethiopian quarters consist of little, blocklike whitewashed houses built on it. "A cluster of hovels," they have been called by one European writer, but I don't think this does them justice. They are like an African or Middle Eastern village, it is true, but to me they seemed clean and neat. The white houses had bright-painted woodwork, and near them stood bright-green pepper trees, growing from amid the roof-tiles. The houses seemed ideal places for study or contemplation.

Outside them the priests appeared to be not doing much. The air in Jerusalem was often chilly, for all the drought and sunshine, and the Ethiopians did not seem keen on going about in it. A better environment, perhaps, was furnished for them by the Jordan Valley — much lower and much warmer, though not far away — where they had another establishment and where I would, in fact, be seeing them shortly. Their Epiphany service would be held beside the Jordan — along with those of the Greeks, the Syrians, and the Copts — on January eighteenth, the same day as the Armenian Christmas Eve. I planned to take those services in — as my long Christmas moved on to its close — and indeed they would give me a better feeling of Christ's life and times than anything thus far.

THE ARMENIAN CHRISTMAS

AND SO ON JANUARY EIGHTEENTH I started, after breakfast, for the Jordan. As conveyance I had an old seven-passenger taxi, belonging to my hotel, and as company I had Fathers Smith and Collins, who wished, as I did, to see the services. Our interests were somewhat different — the Fathers were concerned with fine points of the Eastern liturgies, and I, more superficially, with the general scene — but at least we shared a holiday mood. We had brought picnic lunches and we were looking forward to a nice day in the country — especially in a climate more gentle than the one we were leaving. Jerusalem and Bethlehem, the main theaters of my Christmas so far, are on the Judean Highlands, at an altitude of half a mile. They have a fairly rugged winter, even in times of sunshine and great drought, as this had been. The Jordan Valley, on the other hand, is twelve hundred feet below sea level — the lowest dry land on the earth's surface — and except in big storms it is always balmy there, and fertile with palms, bananas, and citrus trees.

The drop from the Highlands to the Valley is a sharp one, taking but half an hour's drive, on a winding road,

through the Judean Wilderness. Before we reached this
drop, though, we drove past the Old City of Jerusalem —
between it and Gethsemane — then turned east and skirted
the Mount of Olives. We passed within sight of Bethpage
— a little place up near the Mount — and then through the
larger village of Bethany. In Christian history those sites
are connected with Christ's final years on earth. Bethany,
the home of Mary and Martha, is where He sometimes
stayed in His career of preaching. Bethpage is where His
disciples found the donkey for His ride on Palm Sunday.
And from there He rode westward over the Mount of
Olives, down through Gethsemane, and thus into the city.
At Easter time the churches hold special ceremonies in those
sites, as they do in Bethlehem at Christmas. But the services
today would mark an intermediate phase of Christ's life —
when He was thirty years old, and was baptized, and began
to preach after the Holy Ghost had descended on Him.

As we left Bethany the road began to fall, and the little
stone houses became fewer in the landscape, then died out
entirely. Except for occasional spots the country was no
longer habitable on a year-round basis — it had too little
water, that is, to support farms or gardens. The asphalt
road snaked down through tawny hills. Now and then we
saw the flattish dark-brown tent of a Bedouin nomad,
pitched beside a *wadi* or dry stream bed, where a little
water might conceivably be found, and some forage for
the goats. The pickings of this sort were slim, though.
Besides the shower eleven days earlier — at the Greek Orthodox Christmas — there had been one other in the mean-
time, but neither had come near to ending the drought.
We saw hints of green in a *wadi* now and then, but on the
whole the land was dun and dead. The goats and sheep
we saw were gaunt, and they worked hard at ranging for

their food. "The animals are having a bad time all through Jordan," Father Collins said. "I hear they are slaughtering camels down near Aqaba, for lack of water."

We passed near some landmarks on the way — the supposed inn where the good Samaritan put the wounded traveler up, and a supposed tomb of Moses. The latter site is thought genuine only by the Moslem Arabs, I believe — not by Moses' other worshippers, the Jews and Christians — and the former is also questionable, but both point up the fact that the Judean Wilderness is a zone of transit, as well as of nomadic grazing. Christ Himself used to come through it, according to the Gospels, on His way to Jerusalem from Jericho in the Valley.

The Wilderness is also a zone of hermitage. John the Baptist went down into it when abandoning the world. Remains of the Qumran monastery of the Essenes — famous for the Dead Sea scrolls — are in it, too, or in the lower edge of it. Then in the fourth century A.D. — during the great Byzantine development of the Holy Land — many Christian monasteries were founded there, of the ascetic Eastern kind.

Most of these monasteries are gone now from the Wilderness — or are lingering on as scanty ruins — but a few still function in a small way, and I had visited one of them, Mar Saba of the Greek Orthodox, a few days before this Jordan trip. It was a wild and lonely establishment plastered on a cliffside, in a canyon, high up above a little *wadi*. I was shown chapels and common rooms there; and across the way, cut in the facing cliff, I saw many caves where monks had once lived by themselves and meditated. The whole monastery was a complex, random thing, with little rooms, caves, balconies, stairways, roofs, and windows stuck here and there on the cliff like a farflung wasp's nest. It was all wonderfully calm and silent, hanging as it did above the lonely chasm. It seemed very like Tibetan monasteries, indeed, and oddly enough the colors in the chapel murals — rich reds and blacks and golds — seemed Tibetan, too, as did the faint smell of incense there, and the coolness. My glimpse of Mar Saba made me keen to learn more about Greek monasticism, a wish I was to gratify — though more than a year later — by visiting Mount Athos.

Earlier in my Christmas season I had visited Qumran, too, and I had been reading a good deal about it. The place had been fully monastic, I had gathered, in our sense of the word, although the Essenes' objectives had gone beyond the usual monkish one of leading the mystical, ascetic life — they had been actively preparing for a Messiah, that is, and they had also been on the defensive against some hostile, menacing force in their society. This embattledness of their community, in fact — coming as it did around Christ's time — had struck me as being right in tune with the next two thousand years of Palestinian history, with all its religious strife. And the Essenes' stay at Qumran had been ended in that same mood, appropriately, in 70 A.D. by the violence of Titus' legionaries.

When I had gone to Qumran I had found it just a ruin, if a good deal excavated of late. It had stood on a bench — of dry, beige, gravelly earth — in the region where the Judean Wilderness fell down to the Dead Sea, a few miles south of our present goal on the Jordan — I had found it, like Mar Saba, a marvelously calm and peaceful spot — though it looked not down to a chasm, but out on the Dead Sea waves. I had also found it enigmatic, like the rest of the Wilderness. I felt that no modern man had much idea of what thoughts and influences had floated, two thousand years ago, around in that emptiness.*

Today we continued down the black road, anyway, between the dust-brown hills. We passed a sign announcing sea level, then kept on descending. Our big old car swayed dizzily on the curves, but our driver was experienced, and we made good time. He was an Arab Christian named George — belonging to the Greek Orthodox Church — and he knew the program of the day's festivities, as well as how to reach them. We discussed these matters with him, by means of his halting English and the Fathers' Arabic. Then we got down to the valley bottom, which was flat and rich, but also brown now with the drought. We drove northward a few miles, passed through the outskirts of modern Jericho — a dusty, tropical-looking town, much swollen by refugees — and then turned east toward the river, going past gently sloping fields.

The different Churches had different sites on the riverbank, and our first goal was that of the Greek Orthodox. But we were early in getting there — the crowd was only gathering — so we stopped short and turned south, toward the other establishments, to make preliminary calls on them. The road we traveled was a simple dirt one, alive now with a holiday crowd. In less than a mile we passed the Copts' and Syrians' headquarters, then brought up in front of the Ethiopians', where we stopped the car and got out. There was a compound there, with a large white-

---

* At Qumran and Mar Saba I felt — as I was to feel again at Athos — a strong impression of influence from farther east. In the past I had visited monasteries in India, China, the Himalayas, and the Tibetan borderlands; and now I found the atmosphere of those places — and even the details of their arrangements — echoed strikingly in these old establishments of the Judean Wilderness.

plastered building in it — a church and monastery — along with a few small outhouses. We walked up a drive to the monastery and were let in by a tall young Ethiopian priest. We were shown to a reception room with a tile floor, wicker armchairs, and photos on the walls of Ethiopian notables; and soon we were given Turkish coffee while an older priest came to sit and talk with us. The monastery had been built in the nineteen thirties, he told us. "Our king came to the Holy Land and visited the Sacred River," he said. "He saw that our people were sheep without a shepherd, and so he ordered that this church be built." The king in question had been Haile Selassie.

The priest told us also that the monastery had a sizable plantation behind it, down toward the river, and that a procession would pass that way at four in the afternoon. We talked some more, then thanked him and left, saying we would come to their service later. He bowed us out graciously. "We are all brothers in Christ," he said to the Fathers. "Our king Haile Selassie is very famous. He has just made a trip to Europe and America."

On our way back we stopped briefly at the Syrians' place, which was a simple church — rough and informal in the style I had come to think of as Syrian Christian. Its plaster walls had cracks, and in the back of the nave itself some families were picnicking, having evidently spent the night there. They had rugs spread on the floor; and food and refuse, such as orange peels, lay round them. They were friendly in their welcome, but we felt we should get back now, and so we didn't linger — and we passed the Copts up entirely for the present.

When we reached the Greeks' place again we left the car and made our way, through the crowd, toward the

river. A few thousand people were on hand by now,
swarming and picnicking. They all were Arabs, but Christian Arabs, not Moslems, and they wore Western clothing
for the most part. The sky was blue, and the scene was
bright, dusty, and rather hot. Orange and banana peels lay
on the ground. The river, when I reached it, was narrow
and muddy-looking — brown and glinting in the sun —
but flowing at a good speed. Its size did not deserve the
name of river, really — however much its historical importance did — and I think that any girl could have thrown
a stone across it. Its banks were about fifteen feet high, and
steep and bare — muddy toward the bottom and dusty
toward the top. On the top itself an intermittent gray-green
fuzz of brush was growing.

An army bridge — a Bailey bridge, I think — had been
built across the stream, and I walked over this to the eastern side. Beyond the bank there, on the flat ground, the
brush continued, broken now and then by patches of brown
grass. It continued for a few score yards, that is, and then
it met some badlands, almost like those of South Dakota,
rising up. They were as tall as houses — bare, camel-
colored, and rounded — fantastically eroded. Beyond them,
I knew — though I could not see it at the moment — the
Jordan Valley's eastern side swept back and upward to its
wall, the so-called hills of Midian. And beyond the hills
would lie vistas and vistas of desert, then Mesopotamia,
then thousands of further miles of Asia, and no more
Christmas.

I turned back, recrossed the bridge, and once more found
the Fathers. "Traditionally," said Father Smith, "this spot
is where Joshua crossed the Jordan, on his way to Jericho
and the Promised Land." Traditionally too, I gathered, it
must have been thought the most likely site of Christ's

Baptism, for the powerful Greeks were ensconced there, while the weaker Syrians, Copts, and Ethiopians held forth down stream. The Latins evidently shared the rights at this spot, too, for they had a little chapel near where we were standing; and they, like the Greeks, had a big picnic-shed right next to the bank. Both these sheds were of rickety frame construction, with palm-fronds laid on them for roofs. The Greeks had no other structure near the bank, but well away from it — a few hundred yards to the rear, on higher ground — they had a biggish monastery. I could see it in the distance. It was old in design, with crenellated walls, but new in construction, with cement-like hardness, and sharpness, to it.

Noon had passed by now. The moon was well up in the eastern sky; it was more than a half-moon already — getting back toward full, indeed, as I had seen it on the Latin Christmas Eve. The crowd was still inactive — happy and patient — but there were signs of ritual to come. A priest was selling candles on the bank, and a boat with "₿" — the Greek Patriarch's monogram — on its bow lay out in midstream, moored by a rope to either bank. It was a big one, like a lifeboat, with half a dozen rowing seats across it.

Some Arab dancers began a sideshow not far off from me; I could not see them for the crowd around them, but I heard their drums. Then some boy scouts came on the scene, beating drums and blowing bugles. This was about one-thirty, and I was standing on the western bank, right next the palm-roofed shelter of the Greeks. The bank across the way was a mass of brush and people now — the latter peering out through the former like Douanier Rousseau's animals, except that there were many more of them. The shelter beside me was mainly crowded, too, I noticed, but there was also a clear place in it, where some priests and Jordanian soldiers were waiting. Once I heard a lay-man in furious altercation with a soldier there — arguing, I supposed, about whether he should move out of the way.

Later I heard drums and bugles again, and more soldiers came into the shed from the other side, along with a *kawass* or two and several priests. The drums and bugles stopped, and the priests were chanting. I could not see them well through the crowd, but I did make out green and yellow vestments on them, and black cylindrical hats. They chanted a long, long time, while the crowd outside, around me, babbled.

I thought back on how that scene might have looked at Christ's Baptism. A crowd must have been there then, for the Gospels say that people were flocking to be baptized by John. But had it been so dense a crowd? And had the staging been like this? I wondered, as I heard the chanting, interspersed with bells attached to shaken censers.

Anyway the crowd today was made from an enduring ele-ment — humanity. A woman shouted at her little boy, some distance off, and a priest turned round and shushed her. Another woman sat down faintly on the bank. The banks, except for their sloping faces, were thickly packed now, and a stealthy jockeying for good positions was under way. This had its rules as usual. One did not obviously hit a woman or an old man in a tender place. One pretended that some-one else had done it — or that it had been an accident — and meanwhile one slipped into the vacuum it had cre-ated. This was going on a lot, I think, but it was hard to perceive by any sense but touch.

Meanwhile the narrow, muddy stream flowed past be-low us — so narrow, it seemed, that a man could plunge across it without swimming. It was straight where it went between the crowd, then below that it bent sharply to the left, without widening. I saw that people in the crowd were handing bottles of river water round. Then I saw a man drawing water in a small tin pail to fill these bottles; he had the pail on a string, and he would throw it out in the stream and let it sink before pulling it in. Later I saw a bottle floating down on the current — someone had dropped it from the bridge, perhaps. The crowd threw clods or pebbles at it, and throughout its course it was followed by little splashes, till it vanished round the bend.

There was a small rowboat in the stream, besides the big one moored there, and it was very active, taking now a priest and now a layman somewhere. Later Fathers Smith and Collins, who were not with me at this time, told me they had seen a baby baptized from the boat by immersion, and also an older couple baptized by sprinkling. I missed these events, but I did see the small boat take a priest out to the larger one for a while, then later take a layman out and leave him there to pull the large boat in, hand over hand by the rope attached to my shore. After that it lay beneath us, in the shallows.

At twenty to three there was a flurry of vesting in the shelter. People in the crowd straightened up, and there was a movement toward the boat. I saw some priests down near it now, and soon five of them got in, along with a soldier and three laymen. Then a long procession left the shelter, of priests all chanting, and carrying flowers, candles, and religious instruments. They went down the bank and into the boat, and suddenly it was full. It had more than two dozen people in it — laymen, women, and policemen as well as priests. They stood there awkwardly, finding their balance, and a priest on the bank tried to push them off with an oar. He could not budge the boat, though; it was stuck fast. Then three women were made to get down from the bow (though two others, in the stern, remained), and so the craft was lightened, and they got it away. They took it out past midstream and let it hang there on the ropes, the passengers standing or moving gingerly — one passenger was a cameraman, and he had a hard time changing position to take pictures.

The small, strong-faced Greek Patriarch was not on hand today. The chief man was an elder prelate, dressed in red, whose hair and beard were whitish. He chanted from a book, held by two young priests in yellow. They held candles, too. He chanted a long time, and in the course of this the boat once listed heavily to port. The police got the passengers, hastily, to trim it back again. Then more chanting. The prelate wore spectacles, and in time his helpers took them off, and he bent over, holding a cross — to represent Christ Himself — and flowers; and he dipped them in the water several times. Then he stood up, and caps and guns went off in the crowd, and drums and bugles sounded, and the boat came slowly back to shore.

The crowd began to move. I did not wait to link up with the Fathers, but started down the stream alone — we had arranged a rendezvous, with the car, at the Ethiopian service. I left the throng of Orthodox behind me, and for some time I walked in solitude, through scattered trees along the bank. Then I came amid those trees to groups of Syrian Christian picnickers. I did not see the Syrian service — it had ended, I found out — but later I did come on the Coptic one. I found a few Coptic priests down by the water, on a flight of steps there — a *ghat*, the Indians would have called it, and the scene reminded me of *ghats* at Benares on the Ganges. The priests were vested, and they wore the Coptic headgear, of red *tarbooshes* bound with turban-cloths of black. They were passing a book to and fro among them and chanting from its text — the words were old Egyptian, I believe, and the subject was the Gospel story of the Baptism — of how Christ came up from the water, and the Holy Ghost descended as a dove, and God's voice was heard, saying, "This is my beloved Son, in whom I am well pleased."

The scene looked Eastern to me, and I think it was Eastern inwardly as well, with its focus on the grown Messiah's enlightenment — not unlike Gautama's enlightenment, indeed, beneath the Bo tree at Budh Gaya, which is deemed the starting-point of Buddhism. The interest in the water seemed Eastern, too, not European. I have mentioned India in this connection, and lately I have also read that the Christian Epiphany derives from an ancient water-ceremony on the Nile. Again, these hints of faraway influences — however vague to historians — can be persuasive to beholders on the scene; and that is what they were to me. I felt that my Christmas had slipped far from the Western world. Of course it never had been Western in the popular way. I had been Christmas-going for twenty-three days now, and in the course of this I had not seen a Santa Claus, a reindeer, a holly-wreath, a plum-pudding, or a gift-wrapped package. On December twenty-fourth, it is true, I had heard some European carols and seen some bunting on a pine tree. But the tree had not been pointed or symmetrical, and anyway that had been long ago. Now, at this stage, I was walking by a Sacred River and listening to praises of Christ's spiritual, not His natural, Birth.

The bearded priests sang on, down by the waterside, and again I thought they had a sad, exhausted look, and I wondered if it came from the Church's low estate in Egypt. I didn't stay there long, though, but left and went on down the river, walking through dust and eucalyptus trees and palms. It was warm and pleasant in the slanting sun there, and the river meandered narrowly — and smoothly, like a brown mirror — between reedy banks.

It curved slowly round a big flat field, where a dozen people were bending over as if weeding. I followed the curve around, then passed through another clump of trees, then came on a *ghat* that seemed to be the Ethiopians'. It was a flight of concrete steps with iron railings, and near its top there was a paved terrace and a little concrete building. Not much was doing there. A dozen people were standing round, only two of whom — a black-robed nun and a little girl — looked dark and Ethiopian.

I walked away from the bank, inland, and soon I saw the white monastery, which we had visited, standing off on a little rise. Four children were coming from that direction, across the fields, bearing three straight chairs. I sauntered toward them, through open fields — toward what seemed to be the Ethiopians' plantation. Fruit trees and other plants were ranged in order there, and they looked well irrigated and green.

As I walked along I heard a bell ring in the monastery, and then I saw a procession coming from it, led by a series of black-robed figures. They came slowly onward, and I went slowly in their direction. The plantation, when I got there, had cauliflowers and many other vegetables in it. Also palm trees, and it was under these that I met the procession, though I stood well out of its way. First came several black-robed priests, walking quietly in single or double file. Then came two pairs of colorfully vested ones, the leaders bearing a cross and bell, and the others bearing censers. They were followed by a dozen more in black, some bearing objects too. They all walked softly through the verdure, and easily, with random intervals between them.

I followed them down toward the river, where in time they gathered on the terrace by the *ghat*. It was an enclosure, really, with a low wall round it; and as a landward entrance it had an archway, now decorated with a cross, some greenery, and a painting of the Baptism scene. A few score people — mainly Arabs and Arab children — had gathered round the place by now, but it was still a quiet occasion, close to nature. The fields behind us, toward the plantation, were peaceful too, except for a couple of hunters who crossed once in the middle distance, carrying guns. On the other side, beyond the river, some badlands rose as they had across from the Greeks. They were naked and round, made of impacted clay — smooth dry mud, it was — and they glowed a brownish-orange in the waning sun.

A Syrian priest — a guest, it seemed — came into the enclosure, but all the others there were Ethiopians. Most wore black robes with either soft black caps or hard cylindrical ones, like the Greeks'. There were a couple of nuns there too — or such I took them to be — and their gowns were also black, and their caps of black velvet. Of the vested priests, two wore robes of gold brocaded on red; a third wore gold on green; and the fourth a mixture of golds together.

The priests read aloud from a book, taking turns and going on and on, in the quiet scene. Father Collins had appeared by now, and I asked him if it was the Gospels being read. "Yes, it must be," he answered. "But perhaps Old Testament prophecies as well. Because the reading lasts so long." He could not follow the liturgy's words — I think they were in Geez or Ethiopic — but he was familiar with the substance.

The priests read on, and then at length began to chant. They moved position now and then, and now and then they shook their censers, which had bells on them like sleigh-bells. The smell of sandalwood rose up, and it mixed with that of the earth and the growing things.

I was restless on the outskirts, and I wandered round, looking at the muddy river and the green brush and reeds beside it. I went to the little concrete building, but it was empty, and I did not learn its use. I looked at the *ghat* as well. It seemed new, and it went right down to the water, low as that was now. The muddy current lapped against the bottom step.

Then as I stood there two young priests came in my direction. They were holding a little board — nearly square, and a foot or two across — and they proceeded to stick three lighted candles on it, upright. Then they went down the steps, tied the board, by a length of string, to an overhanging piece of brush there, and set it on the water. It lay out on the current like a raft — moored and bobbing a little — while the candles burned and flickered.

I went back to Father Collins and told him what I had seen, but I was hazy on the candles' number. "I think there were three," I said, "but I am not sure."

"Yes," he answered. "There would be three. For the whole Trinity was manifest at the Baptism. The Holy Spirit descended, you remember, and the Lord's voice was heard."

Father Smith had joined us now, and we stood looking at the ceremony, which seemed to be working toward a climax — the chanting had intensified. I noticed a white-haired Ethiopian prelate in the group now. He was dressed rather differently from the others, and I think he was a bishop. He looked unusually kind and dignified, I felt as

I watched him. I also noticed a striking openwork cross, held by a younger priest. It was of metal — bronze, perhaps — and was worked in a sort of basketweave pattern that is called the endless knot in farther Asia and that in Palestine appears in crosses in old Byzantine mosaics. The cross looked exotic to me, even after the gorgeous jeweled ones I had been seeing, of the Greeks and others.

Now presently the white-haired bishop took this cross and started down the steps, to the accompaniment of chanting. He walked down slowly and gracefully, smiling with good humor, as if the ceremony were fun, however solemn. The other priests began to follow him — gracefully, too — in procession; and meanwhile we laymen gathered outside the railings as best we could.

The old bishop continued till he reached the bottom step — I no longer saw the board and candles — and then he bent over and dipped the cross, holding it under the current awhile and waving it back and forth there. Then he stood up again and raised it. He faced about, and the stairway was full of priests now. The old man gave the cross to the lowest one, and then it passed upward from one to the other. And as each priest took it he wiped some water from it and wet his face.

Then the priests withdrew except for two young ones at the bottom. They were holding a brass basin and they filled it from the river. They started slowly upward, too, with the basin between them and the bishop following after. And as they rose the bishop dipped his hands in the basin — again and again — and with them he simply flung drops of water at the multitude. It hit us wet and coolly in our faces, and we all smiled happily, and the bishop did the same. And ministering thus he reached the terrace, where in time the chanting ceased; and the Ethiopians walked back through their plantation while the bell tolled.

George the driver was on the scene now; and he led the Fathers and me to his taxi, and we started home. We went up the dirt road again, to the turn near the Greeks' river bank, and a big crowd was standing around still. We picked two more passengers up there, whom George had promised lifts to. One was a young Greek priest, who spoke no English, and the other was a Greek-Christian Arab woman, a servant in my hotel, who spoke it well, and wittily. She was a character, as we would say, and she chanced to know Fathers Smith and Collins, along with George and myself. She sat beside George in the front now; the Greek priest and I sat on the jump-seats; and the two Catholics sat in the back.

We drove up the inclined plain to Jericho again, then headed south, toward the road that would take us on up through the Wilderness. The sun had set, but dusk had not yet fallen, and we drove along. Then suddenly George bade us look ahead, through the windshield, and there in the distance, above the hills to the Dead Sea's east, a storm was gathering, with big black clouds. "It's like a sandstorm," the woman said, and we all remarked on it. Then as we reached the turn up to Jerusalem we were hit by the wind. It roared around us, and buffeted us; and afterward it stayed with us, up the winding road, as darkness fell.

The Greek priest sat hunched forward as we drove, talking with the Arab woman, mainly, over the back of the front seat — she sat turned half around, to see us all. They talked in Arabic, I think, perhaps with Greek mixed in — I didn't understand it, anyway. From time to time the woman translated something into English for us. She and the priest both thought the storm would bring some rain, apparently, and they held that the Greek rituals today deserved the credit.

This brought on cross-talk, back and forth. What about the Ethiopian rituals then, and the Syrian and the Coptic? And what about the Armenians? Tonight was their Christmas Eve, after all, and their services in Bethlehem must have begun already. The Greeks had had a small rain on their Christmas, one of us said, and now the Armenians would have a big one. And so it went — badinage in the taxi, back and forth, with the woman laughing.

The young Greek priest was untidy looking — his gown not neat, and his hair in a slapdash bun at the back. He spoke morosely to the Arab woman, and she told us that he had joined the Church only recently — and without much training, as is possible with the Orthodox. He was very junior in the Patriarchate, it seemed, and was given onerous tasks there. "He has to work very hard," the woman said. "He works as a guard, sometimes in the Holy Sepulchre and sometimes in the Church of the Nativity, watching out for the Orthodox rights. He works at night, and it never seems to end."

They talked some more, and then the woman laughed. "He said he fought a Catholic priest the other day," she told us, flashing her eyes at the Fathers in the back. "He says he likes the Catholics personally, very much, but his duty requires him to fight with them. Personally, he says, he believes it is all one Church."

She smiled again, and Fathers Smith and Collins smiled, but they refrained from answering. We kept a friendly silence till we reached Jerusalem, and there the wind was blowing hard now.

I cleaned up, had dinner, and set out once more for Bethlehem — again with George. I meant to see at least part of the Armenian services, to round my Christmas out. We reached Manger Square, by the Church of the Nativity, at nine o'clock, and the place was dark and empty now, without the life and bustle I had grown used to in it. The curio shops were shuttered up. The evergreen beside the Square had colored lights still in its branches, but the branches were tossing against the stormy sky. Rain was not falling yet — the flat half-moon shone up there in the blackness — but clouds were up there, too, and the wind in the stone-paved town was blustery.

I went into the Church of the Nativity by its little door. The big nave was empty, dark, and shadowy now, and I kept on through it to the northern transept, the Armenians' territory. That part was lit up, but quiet still. A few lay Armenians were fixing decorations — hanging lamps and doing things like that. A priest was filling the lamps with oil, pouring it from a big long-spouted pot. The stone floor was covered, every inch, with rugs now, too. I went downstairs to the Grotto of the Nativity, and the floor there had likewise been covered with rugs. The Grotto was bright with lamps and candles.

I came back up and hung around the transept awhile, but it was chilly and uneventful there, so I left and went outside, to get a drink. My steps were lonely on the flagstones. I found an Arab tea-house near the Square, up a narrow flight of stairs. The place was warm and bright, and a few dozen men were playing cards in it. I had two glasses of brandy — made by Catholic fathers in the Holy Land — and it warmed me nicely.

When I went back to the church I found more people in the transept. I stood watching them, and soon bells be-

gan to ring, in the direction of the Armenian monastery
— they were in the belfry on its roof. I walked back toward
the church's entrance, and in the big nave I was stopped
by the sound of three *kawasses,* banging their staffs down
loudly on the flagstones. They banged with a metallic beat
and came on slowly.

Then a file of priests, fifteen or twenty strong, came after
them, walking silently and wearing the black Armenian
hoods. Their faces, by and large, were pale, and some of
them wore glasses. They had a severe, intellectual look —
less jolly than the Greeks', for instance. They seemed
quieter and more mysterious. In their black hoods they
went slowly through the darkened nave, with the *kawasses*
banging ahead of them.

They reached the carpeted transept, took places there,
and began to say their liturgy. Later on they sang it, too,
and their ritual unfolded. A couple of the priests had gray
beards — most of them had black ones — and these elders
were now vested in purple. Choir-boys — some in light
gray and some in grayish-blue — gathered beside the priests'
formation. And there was censing, too, along with the
chanting.

The congregation was much smaller, and more decorous,
than those on the Greek and Latin Christmas Eves. It numbered about two hundred people, and it fitted nicely in the
transept. Almost everyone seemed to be Armenian, except
for some Arab policemen. Most had come from Jordanian
Jerusalem, I think, but a few must have been from Israel
— I know that crossing had been allowed on this Christmas, as on the Greek and Latin ones, though I think far
fewer had taken the opportunity.

The time drew on toward midnight, and I went down
to the Grotto again. It was warm and cozy with the lights,

and many people were there, some worshipping. I came back up, and the Armenians' space was fuller. The Anglican Archbishop had arrived, with a party of other British guests, and these were seated on a row of chairs. Some of the priests had changed their black, too, for red-and-white-striped vestments.

Just before twelve I heard bells ringing — on the Armenian monastery again — and then I heard a *kawass* in the nave. I went that way and saw the tall Muhafez — the Military Governor — being led in. He wore a white tie and tails, with many orders, and he looked impressive as the *kawass* banged him through the big dark empty space.

Back at the service the chanting was intense now. All the priests were vested in red and white — a gay, almost peppermint effect it gave them — and soon they proceeded down into the Grotto, with the notables behind them. I did not follow there myself, but stood awhile in the apse to hear the chanting. A young Armenian came and spoke to me. "The singing is very sweet," he said. "You must listen to the rhythm in the voices. A German expert has called it the best singing in the Middle East."

The young man was eager, and I smiled and nodded, though I am no judge of things like that. The singing did sound good, but whether it was better than the Greeks' or Latins', or the others', I cannot say. Anyway I listened awhile, then took my leave, and went back through the howling darkness to Jerusalem.

An Armenian friend, a layman, had asked me to a party on Christmas night, in Saint James' monastery. I looked forward to it gladly, especially on Christmas day when I woke up, for the storm had broken earlier with great force. The rain was lashing and lashing against my window, and

by lunchtime the flag on the Indonesian consulate, which
was in my vista, had blown half away. The neon sign on a
neighboring hotel had partly blown off too. The rain came
into my room all day through cracks, and on the ground
outside it ran in streams.

The party, after dark, was warm ånd cheering, if hard
to get to — we dashed head-down through the showering,
deluged medieval courtyards of Saint James', over flagstones deep in water. Inside we sat in a crowded, bright-lit,
vaulted room, where I drank Christmas brandy and watched
Armenian folk-dancing. The music seemed very Western
to me, compared with Arab music, and I remarked on this.
"Yes," my host answered. "It *is* Western, and we are Western, too." Which surprised me, for Armenia lies so deep
in Asia geographically.

In a while my host began to tell about the organization
that was giving the party tonight — of which he was a leading member. It was a political group, apparently, devoted
nowadays to keeping the Church in Soviet Armenia from
influencing the diaspora too much. "We have three clubs
in our community," he said, "and this is the most right-
wing of them, and the strongest." It was the club of the so-
called Dashnaks, I learned, and it was several decades old.
"In the past we helped set up a new Catholicos, or head of
the Church, in Lebanon," my friend said "— a rival to the
one at Etchmiadzin in the Soviet. And now we are having a
struggle right here at Saint James', to block the confirmation in Jerusalem of a so-called Patriarch-elect, who belongs
to the Etchmiadzin party."

The story of this struggle was a long one. I heard a lot
of it that night, and later I heard more from other Armenians, including Father Turusian — he belonged to the
anti-Dashnak, or Etchmiadzin, or legitimist camp, and he

had been working in Jordan for its interests. Jordan was involved politically, indeed, for King Hussein's government had banished the pro-Etchmiadzin Patriarch-elect, and the latter was now an exile, living in England. Meanwhile the Armenians in Jerusalem had no Patriarch, though they were entitled to one — the graybeards leading the service on their Christmas Eve had been but senior priests.

I don't know what has happened in that issue since I left Jerusalem. Nor can I judge its merits, or dwell on it here in further detail — it would make a whole new story. But it seems worth mentioning as proof that the old schismatic tendency in Church affairs — and the mixing into them of force and politics — is still alive and current.

Also, of course, the story was part of that evening — of the Dashnaks' Christmas. The setting for it was a fit one, too, as we saw the dancing and heard the music beneath the massive vaults and arches of that medieval monastery, which was a fortress, potentially, as well. It had sheltered the Armenians in ancient times and also modern ones — a decade earlier, my friend said, in the Arab-Israeli war of 1948, the Armenian community had shut itself in there. "Five thousand people lived here then," he said, "eating stored food and drinking water from the cisterns that lie under us. We closed the gate and let in neither Jews nor Arabs unless we wanted to — they could not break in. And we are ready to do it again if trouble comes."

On Christmas night this readiness was apparent in the masonry, but not in the people's actions. The people danced and sang and had a merry holiday, while outside the rain poured down in sheets. It was still pouring when we left the place, along toward midnight. It poured till morning, too, and all the next day, and for several days thereafter, throughout the Holy Land. It rained down on the just and unjust; on Moslems, Jews, and Christians; on the orthodox and heretical alike. It stormed all winter, in fact, and Palestine got its wettest season in at least three decades. And long before Easter the land was green again.

PART TWO

HOLY WEEK AT MOUNT ATHOS

Inset map:

GREECE

Salonika

ATHOS PENINSULA

AEGEAN SEA

Athens

N

Main map:

Cape Arapes

Terissos

A E G E A N

Chilandari +

+ Esphigmenou

Vatopedi

+ Pantocrator
+ Stavronikita

Karyes
+ Saint Andrew's skete
+ Iviron

Xeropotamou
Daphni
Simonos Petra

S E A

Great Lavra

Dionysiou +

MOUNT

Karoulia
cliffs

ATHOS

+ Kapsokalyvia

MT. ATHOS
PENINSULA

holy week at mount athos

At Easter a year later I reached Mount Athos, to see more of the Greek monasticism I had glimpsed at Mar Saba in the Wilderness. Or, more strictly, it was a bit before Easter; it was the eve of Palm Sunday. I went there then and stayed till Easter morning — throughout Holy Week, which is the great moment of the Athonite year. The monks held services continually that week, and I went to them now and then. But I went less often than I might have, because I was more interested, on this trip, in the round of monastic life than in the liturgical — and ecclesiastical — sides of religion that had engrossed me in the Holy Land. Athos has fewer monks, by far, than it had in the past, yet it is still a functioning monastic realm of great extent — the biggest in the world, most likely, since the smashing of Tibetan Buddhism — and when there one absorbs its influence through all that happens, however commonplace. One neglects history in favor of the daily scene.

"Mount Athos" is a peninsula, as well as a mountain rising from its end. The peninsula is thirty miles long by a few miles wide, and it runs into the Aegean from Macedonia in North Greece. For a thousand years — since 963 — it has been given over to monasteries of the Orthodox Church, being ruled by them as a half-autonomous state, first under the Byzantine Empire, then under the Turks, and now under Greece.

The monks' rule keeps Mount Athos inviolate by their standards, and no woman may set foot there. But men are welcome, and so on that Saturday afternoon — before Palm Sunday — I boarded a caïque, or small Greek sailboat (with an auxiliary motor), at the village of Ierissos, which is the jump-off for Athos on the peninsula's north side. There were four passengers besides myself. One was John Yiannias, a Greek-American theology student who had come with me from Athens. The others — two Swedes and an American — had been on the bus that morning from Salonika, the nearest city, and we had joined forces en route. We had lunched in Ierissos and then walked down to the beach, where the caïque was waiting. The beach was of coarse brown sand, and a plank ran up from it to the boat's gunwhale. We climbed this with our baggage; then the engine started and we were off.

It was a good spring day — sunny, gusty, chilly, and lazy all at once. The sea was a thick, bright Mediterranean blue, with whitecaps on it here and there. The land was green, but misting out to grayish in the distance. At first we couldn't see Mount Athos, or the main body of its peninsula, for they were screened by a subpeninsula — a spur — that ran out a few miles to the north. Our first job was to get round this, and the caïque chugged away at it.

Meanwhile we passengers talked and looked about us. In the fifth century B.C., Xerxes, the Persian conqueror, dug a canal across the peninsula near Ierissos in order that his

ships, descending on lower Greece, might bypass the Mount
Athos headland, where an earlier Persian fleet had wrecked
itself. Now we looked for this canal and asked the two-
man crew about it, and they pointed to the spot — a few
miles east of Ierissos it was, beside a village.

We chugged on and drew nearer to the spur. It was
craggy, with green brush on it like chapparal. Two caïques
were fishing by the shore, with gulls above them. We passed
them and bore on to the rocky point, and in time we went
around it, cutting close. Then Mount Athos stood before
us, conical and dim — almost invisible — in the hazy distance. Again the peninsula leading up to it was green —
dark green in the foreground, then paler, then almost a
pearly gray. Beaches gleamed along its shoreline — distant
beyond the sea, above which flocks of ducks or other birds
were seen in flight at times. They looked like masses of
black dots, low down above the water and moving steadily.

On the Athonite peninsula — as I had been reading —
there are twenty monasteries and many lesser institutions,
all scattered about in the green hilly wilderness. Our goal
now was Vatopedi, a big monastery half-way along the
northern coast, but before reaching it we passed by others.
The first of these was Chilandari, a monastery of the Serbs.
It stood inland, tucked in a valley, and all of it we really
saw was its boathouse, and some storehouses, down by the
water.

Soon after that we passed a Greek monastery, Esphigmenou, which stood on the shore itself, beside a beach. It
was like a castle, with high stone walls and battlements. It
had red roofs, and a green hill stood behind it. A cloud of
white smoke rose near it from the beach, and our captain
said the monks would be burning driftwood and flotsam
there, to tidy up for Holy Week.

We passed on — close to the land by now — and saw other signs of life. Once there was a little stone house by the shore, with cultivated land around it. Then there was a white church on a cliff. Then there were walls of old terraces by the lonely coast. Then just beyond them was another church, amid remnants of a garden.

The water was clear, and we looked deep into its greenness. The air was clear, too, and the wind was dying. It was balmy as we moved along. Then we went round a point and saw Vatopedi, across a cove. It seemed like a village at first, with a few large buildings in it and a tower. Behind it rose a wooded ridge, and over that the top of Mount Athos itself appeared. This stood out clearly now: a peak of light, bare, craggy rock, with streaks of snow on it. Vatopedi was straight below it, and we were speeding there on the smooth water.

A long beach lay at the shore, with many separate buildings near it — brightly colored for the most part, showing as patches of blue and red and white. Above them rose a slope, with olives and fruit trees; then came the monastery itself. On closer view it was less like a village and more like something organized or institutional — a college, say, or a medieval fortress-town. The monastery was set on a high stone wall, around which were gardens and rows of cypress trees. The wall went up sheer for twenty feet or more, and above it were horizontal lines of windows and balconies, tier over tier. Much of this part was painted red, and there were also pinks and whites in it. The horizontality was striking — windows in long, long bands, like strips of paper above each other on a screen. Some of the monastery roofs were slate-gray, and these were sprinkled with a yellow-golden moss. The colors sparkled in the sun and stillness.

We tied up at a concrete jetty there, on which some men — a policeman and other laymen — were standing. They were quiet, and they didn't break the calmness of the place. We heard a rooster crow, and it was very clear. We went ashore, talked with the men a moment, then pushed on up the slope to the monastery. We walked on flagstones, past roses and blooming fruit trees. Big stacks of cordwood were piled around there, too, and mules were bringing timbers down to a warehouse.

Inside the gate we were met by a monk called the *archondaris,* or guestmaster — the monasteries of Athos take guests in readily, without notice, and each has a guestmaster to care for them. Like other Greek monks, this one had long hair, a beard, and a black cylindrical hat, but he wore a sort of duster — for working — over his black habit. He led us up through the central courtyard, then upstairs and to the guests' reception room, which looked out above the shore by which we had come. Vatopedi ranks second, in prestige, among the Athonite monasteries, and it also happens to be the most modernized and luxurious of them. It is nearly a thousand years old, fundamentally, but some of its inner fittings suggest a Victorian club. This reception-room was spacious, and it had stuffy furniture, ornately painted walls, and big framed photographs of notables, including the King and Queen of Greece. It also had an electric chandelier, but Vatopedi's generator, we were told, had broken down some time ago.

We waited awhile, then the guestmaster brought refreshments on a tray — five little cups of Turkish coffee, five little saucers of orange-peel in syrup — with spoons — and five big tumblers of water. We downed our portions thankfully, then he left, and we waited some more. Besides being lavish, the room was well kept up. The windows were clear as crystal, and I went and stood by one, looking down on the slope above the waterfront. It was half past five now, and mules were standing here and there below, resting and feeding with nosebags on. Some had bells on their necks as well, and these sounded occasionally, as they moved.

Also down below were the roses, the fruit trees, the olives, and the slate roofs of various outbuildings, with their golden moss. Water was running and gurgling down there, too, through stone pools and irrigation channels. Outside the window, swallows were darting in the air, and mewing, and there were larger birds in the scene below them — doves, turkeys, chickens, even peacocks. The doves cooed; the turkeys gobbled; the mule-bells tolled; the water sang in its channels; and apart from such sweet noises all was quiet.

The guestmaster came and said our rooms would not be ready for a while, and after that we went out to the courtyard. This was as big, perhaps, as a small urban square. But it was not level; it sloped down toward the sea, and its upper side was two or three stories higher than its lower. It was wholly paved with dark-gray flagstones — tending to become steps in places — and in their cracks were grass and other greenery. The sides of the courtyard, mainly living quarters, were strongly horizontal again — despite the slope — with long rows of windows and balconies. There was a good deal of light blue in the painting, interspersed with the red, the white and the stone-color. The whole place was gay and bright — almost toy-like in its gaiety. It was like a pleasure-dome or palace. And in the court were fruit trees, a well, a fine old bell-tower, a chapel or two, a refectory, and a church, all small in scale and exquisite. The buildings were locked at that hour, and we couldn't get into them; some monks were passing to and fro — old ones, for the most part, wearing the usual black habits and black stovepipe hats — and we asked them for admission, but to no avail. Yet there was much to see from outside. The church's porch had Byzantine murals on it, recalling those at Mar Saba. And its interior had other murals, and so did the refectory's; and we glimpsed these through the windows.

At dusk we were called to dinner, or supper, in the guest quarters. The meal was light because of the Lenten fast, now drawing to its climax. Meat, fish, and dairy products are ruled out in Lent on Athos. Wine is, too, on most occasions. So is olive-oil, a mainstay of Greek cooking. What is left is meager, and what we got that night was typical — only bean soup, potatoes, and dry bread.

A German boy scout, in his late teens, was also at the table, along with two Greek guests. We talked quietly with them and turned in early afterward, not going to a seven-hour church service — a vigil connected with Christ's coming sacrifice — that was being held that night. We had a sound sleep instead, and a quiet one, in good linen on good beds, though the quarters were a little chilly — the walls were of thick masonry, and cold still from the winter.

When we awoke it was Palm Sunday, and then we did go to church, after being given, as breakfast, another round of Turkish coffee, sweets, and water. The church was small, but splendid. It was full of candlelight, glitter and gilt — gilt metals and gilt carvings everywhere. There were candlesticks taller than a man. There were scores of icons placed around, and the walls themselves were covered with religious murals in the Byzantine style — they were mainly red and gold and black in color, again recalling Mar Saba.

Though small in plan, the church was lofty, and the murals went right up to the top — to the crowning dome, from which the Byzantine conception of Christ as Panto-crator — the Almighty — looked down. (This is a stern conception of Our Lord — expressing, so to speak, the austere scrutiny of Heaven — and it normally fills the dome in Orthodox churches. It is a concept far different from the tender Christ of Western art.)

The monks and visitors stood, for the most part, in stalls around the church's edge, and the floor itself was free. It was made of black, white, and red marble, now worn with age, and today it was strewn with green bay leaves, which in Northern Greece are substituted for palm fronds — those not being readily available there. We all held branches of the bay as well. There was a smell of incense in the church, and the Byzantine liturgy was being sung — antiphonal, without polyphony or accompanying instruments — only voices answering each other, and very beautiful. It sounded much like what I had heard in Bethlehem, though today not the Nativity, but Christ's final ride, was being celebrated.

Some Greek laymen were in church — workers, I gathered, on the monastery's holdings — and after the service we were all taken up to a sitting-room, looking high out over the sea again, for more coffee and more sweets. This room, too, had the marks of nineteenth-century grandeur. It had sofas, upholstered armchairs, small tables, photo albums, guestbooks with old signatures, and more photos on the walls — yard-high portraits, some were, framed in gilt.

We downed our refreshments and talked a little with the monks, but we didn't linger; we were due to catch

another boat soon, and we hoped to see the monastery's
treasures before leaving. This we did, though superficially.
First an old monk showed us the library. It was in a tower
in the monastery's corner — beneath its balcony the stone
wall dropped some fifty feet to the ground outside. From
glass cabinets the monk took out old manuscripts on parch-
ment, some beautifully illuminated — hand copies of
things like the Psalms and Gospels, going back to early
centuries of the Church. There were rare printed books
as well, among them many big old folios. The librarian
opened them and showed them, and meanwhile we talked
with him. He said he was seventy and had come to Vatopedi
in 1906. There had been a hundred and thirty monks in
residence then, he added, but now there were less than
fifty. This was a story we would hear throughout Mount
Athos — of monks growing old and passing, and few young
ones to take their place.

Yet our next guide was an exception to the trend — a
young, red-bearded monk who showed us icons and relics
in the church. He seemed vigorous and intelligent, and he
said he had come to Vatopedi only a few years earlier. He
showed us some lovely things, including the only wall
mosaics that exist now on Mount Athos; they were in the
main church and had bright gold backgrounds. He showed
us old icons, too, but we couldn't dwell on them, for our
boat was sighted in the cove and we were summoned.

Our first caïque had been hired especially, but this second was a jitney one, which made a scheduled run each
morning out of Ierissos. We were taking it as far as another
monastery, called Iviron, a few miles farther along the
coast, from where we planned to travel inland to Karyes,

the Athonite capital. We were supposed to register at Karyes within twenty-four hours of reaching the peninsula, and this program would allow that.

The caïque had other passengers, both monks and lay-men. Again we followed the shore, and again we came to intervening monasteries — two of them — but this time we stopped at them, for passengers or freight. Both places had landings at the waterside. The first, called Pantocrator, had a little basin there, with a narrow rocky entrance and stone boathouses, and the monastery itself was near it. The second, Stavronikita, was perched a good deal higher — straight up on a craggy ridge. Both places had features that I was coming to see as typical, including stone towers — which stood up almost like chess castles — and many little balconies, or bay windows, jutting out from living quar-ters into the void. The land we saw was much as yesterday's had been. "Mount Athos" was turning out to be a long stretch of hilly woodland, with the mountain itself still in the distance.

Iviron is a big monastery, but after reaching it we stayed only for lunch and a brief look around. Many of the monks were sleeping, after long services the night be-fore, but the guestmaster, a pleasant man, was there to greet us. First he brought refreshments on a tray — five pieces of Turkish delight this time, five tumblers of water, and five little glasses of *raki,* a clear strong liquor tasting of anise. The drinking of *raki,* at least by travelers, did not seem outlawed in the fast. We found it continually in our week on Athos — the monks distilled it themselves, they said, from the fermented residue of their wine-presses. There was a ritual of hospitality — traditionally Greek, I think — which we met with every time we reached a monastery. A monk would bring a tray, and on it would be, for each guest, a glass of water, a sweet or *"glyco,"* and a shot of *raki* or a Turkish coffee or both. The formula was based on long experience, and it made a most effective freshener. One monk warned us against drinking water without *raki* when we were hot and tired, and I think he was speaking out of ancient wisdom. The *glyco* in the combination seemed important, too. Sometimes it was Turkish delight, sometimes candied orange peel, and sometimes a spoonful of jam or jelly, made by the monks themselves and delicately flavored. Always it revived our energies.

After these refreshments at Iviron, the guestmaster gave us a lunch of bread, unflavored noodle soup, and olives (olive-oil is taboo in the Orthodox Lent, but olives themselves are not, by one of those anomalies that seem common in the rules of fasting). We didn't sit long over the meal, and after it we were shown the church and some of its icons. In shape the church was almost exactly like Vatopedi's — small but soaring loftily — and the fittings gave much the same impression. There was more blue in the murals, though, along with the reds and golds and blacks, and the gilt had less dazzle than Vatopedi's. But the whole thing was rich enough, although the court outside the church, and the monastery generally, seemed poor and run down.

The name Iviron, I found out, means that the monastery was once staffed and supported largely by "Iberians," or Georgians of what is now South Russia. That tie was ended centuries ago, and today Greek monks — but not many of them — man the place. Iviron has one of the best reputations on Mount Athos, but the going seems to be hard for it — we saw tangled weeds in the court, and unkemptness generally, and felt an air of loneliness. The place is said to have a fine old library, but it was locked when we were there, and we felt we shouldn't stay long.

We started up the road for Karyes in the early afternoon — the five of us together still, all walking and carrying our bags and knapsacks. The road was actually a mule-track, its surface roughly cobbled and wide enough, perhaps, to take a jeep. It wound uphill along a stream — now high above this, now descending to it. The sun was warm, but the stream was babbling coolly, and birds were singing in the brush around us — it was early spring there, with the leaves just starting. We met few other travelers, and the journey took us something over an hour, going easily, with pauses.

Karyes that Sunday afternoon was small and quiet — the smallest and stillest capital, perhaps, on earth. It lay on a wooded hillside, and from its center rose a church, called the Protaton, that is nearly a thousand years old. Next to this stood a new building, headquarters of the "Holy Community," a monkish body that rules Mount Athos insofar as the latter is autonomous. There was also a square by the church, and through this passed a cobbled road that might be called a street for a hundred yards of its length — beyond which, at both ends, it frayed off to a network of rustic lanes.

These lanes, as we soon discovered, were sometimes cobbled and sometimes in plain dirt, and often they ran between high stone walls. They led to monastic establishments in the neighborhood and also to houses, among which were the so-called *konakia* of the twenty Athonite monasteries — the residences where live their delegates to the Holy Community, along with any other of their monks who may be in Karyes on business. The houses were of stone, for the most part, and they were in quiet garden settings, with fruit trees, cypresses, and the like nearby. There were also groves of hazels here and there — the name Karyes means "hazels." These trees, or shrubs, were about the size of alders, and they stood in regular clumps amid green grass.

The surroundings of Karyes were peaceful as any village, and the center was peaceful, too. Along its one street were a hotel; two restaurants; the shops of a barber, a tailor, and a cobbler; and two or three souvenir-stores; but all these were small and primitive, and anything but loud. There were no automobiles or other engines. No radios were allowed, and no musical instruments whatever. Smoking was not allowed in the square by the church. Nor was singing, whistling, or shouting. Nor was the wearing of hats, or the riding of mules or other animals. No women or children were in the town, hence few frivolities and no soprano voices. We saw some idlers in the square and frequent passers-by — both monks and laymen — and they hailed each other murmurously. The clatter of the outside world seemed far away.

The Greek nation, which has suzerainty over Athos, is represented in Karyes by a Governor and some uniformed police. Our first move on arriving was to go to these police, and to show them passes we had brought from Athens. In turn they gave us other passes, and we took these to the Holy Community's buildings, where we had to turn them in and get still others. There was a delay in this, and while we waited a monk showed us round the place — it was Sunday, but a few monks were on hand and also a few lay servants, the latter wearing berets with the Holy Community's badge on them (a double-headed Byzantine eagle, this flanked by the letters A and O, for "Ayion Oros," or "Holy Mountain," another name for Athos).

Upstairs in the building was a large room, and the monk told us that the Holy Community meets in it twice weekly. There was an elongated horseshoe table there, with twenty chairs around it, and a desk, for a secretary, in the open end. Then off to one side, on a dais, was a throne for the chief executive, who presides. Its back was wooden and nicely carved, with the Byzantine eagle on it again (the Byzantine Empire has been dead five centuries, but many of its forms — and much of its mentality, one gathers — live on at Athos). The monk told us that the chief executive is drawn, in yearly rotation, from one of the five leading Athonite monasteries — among which Vatopedi and Iviron are numbered — and that three other monks, drawn in rotation from the other fifteen monasteries, serve with him on a sort of executive committee. Thus each monastery has a delegate in the executive every five years, and meanwhile the delegates of all twenty sit together in what can be called the legislature — except that it is more than that, for it tries judicial cases, too. Nowadays, I gathered, its jurisdiction is limited to small matters, like disturbances of the peace; greater cases are tried by the civil courts in Salonika. But there seems to be no appeal from the Community's decisions in its fields of competence.

In time our passes came. They were good for five days, and they directed all the monasteries to take us in during that period. Each was signed by all four members of the executive committee, and I gathered that these officials exercise their rights punctiliously — even jealously — in other ways as well. Each is said to have a key to the treasury, which cannot be unlocked without all four of them. And the Community's official stamp is also made in four parts, which must be given up and screwed together before a document can be validated.

I had brought a letter to the Governor, and John Yiannias and I next went to call on him — his office was five minutes distant by a quiet lane, in a *konaki* of a monastery. The Governor himself was out, but we had a talk with his secretary, who also took us for a stroll.

We asked the secretary about the Holy Community — its politics and economics — for I had been getting more and more curious about these things. He told us that the Community is under Greek suzerainty in material questions, but in spiritual ones is under the Orthodox Patriarch at Constantinople, or Istanbul. Twice a year, for instance, the Community holds an extraordinary meeting, in which abbots or other leading members of the monasteries take part, instead of their ordinary delegates; this makes basic decisions, and if on worldly matters they must be ratified by Athens, if on spiritual ones by Constantinople.

The Community has a good income in its own right, the secretary said, which helps preserve its autonomy. It levies a three per cent duty on all the imports and exports of Athos. It also has a monopoly of the trade in certain commodities — among them meat and tobacco — within its borders. Then beyond that it may call on the separate monasteries for help if need be, though in practice it doesn't do so now.

Some of the monasteries are poor, he went on, but some are rich. Some do a good business, especially, in exporting timber — most of Greece is deforested, but Athos is not. Some also sell wine, olives, and hazel-nuts. Many had great landholdings elsewhere in the past, but these are largely gone now. Some lands were in Russia, Bulgaria, and other countries now Communist, and those have been expropriated. Others were in Greece, and those have been largely taken over by the government, to settle refugees on — more than a million Greeks were repatriated, mainly from Turkey, in the early nineteen twenties, and were badly short of living room on their arrival. These refugees are still on the lands, and the Greek government is paying the monasteries rent for them, although the payments lapsed in the Second World War and are still not back to normal. Athens is discussing that question with the monasteries, apparently, and is also forgiving them certain taxes such as laymen pay — taxes on the real estate, for instance, that some of them hold in Salonika.

The inner Athonite economy sounded feudal as the secretary told of it. The twenty monasteries hold their land in perpetuity, I understood him to say, but much of it is farmed out to lesser institutions, the most important of which are called *sketae* — establishments that may be as big as monasteries themselves — and *kellia*, which are smaller, often having no more than three monks in them. (There are still smaller units on Athos, too, right down to hermitages in caves.) The *sketae* and *kellia* hold their land simply as fiefs of the monasteries, it seems.

The labor on Mount Athos, in theory, is done by monks on a communal system. But their numbers are dwindling now, and much is really done by laymen. There are somewhat over seventeen hundred monks left on the peninsula, according to the secretary, and the lay population is a little bigger than that, though shifting seasonally — there have been more than ten thousand monks on Athos at times in the past.

The prevalence of lay workers entails cash transactions, of course — as does the sale of timber and the like — but still such business is at a minimum. Aside from what the secretary told us, we experienced a good deal of the cashless life ourselves, during the week, in connection with our food and lodging. The monasteries never charged for putting us up. They accepted "candle" money if we gave it to them, but we were not obliged to do so, and there was no understanding of what the amount should be. I got the impression, too, that the monasteries dispense a good deal of straight charity, as well as receiving it. Often their dealings have no price system in our sense.

Our Swedish companions left Karyes that Sunday afternoon, but the other American stayed there overnight with us. His name was John Yohannan, and he was associate professor of English at the College of the City of New York — in Greece temporarily, on a Fulbright fellowship. The three of us shared a room in the Karyes hotel, which was primitive, but passable. A wonderful chorus of peepers sang out behind the hotel in the evening. They were the loudest I have ever heard, I think, and they harmonized well with the spring moisture — Karyes was a gushy place, with water running through it everywhere.

The hotel's cook was under the Lenten restrictions. He could give us no meat, he said; he promised to send out and find some eggs, but never did; and in the end what we had for dinner — in the privacy of our room — was salt codfish, smothered in garlic and served along with greens and bread. We also had some wine. Again we turned in early, and again we slept well in the quiet; and for breakfast we had tea and bread with honey.

The Governor was on hand the next morning, and John Yiannias and I went to see him in the *konaki*. He turned out to be a small, middle-aged, blue-eyed, energetic, intelligent-looking man, and his office was informal, like a study in a country house. I asked him about the relations of Church and State on Athos, but he brushed this question aside and began talking, instead, about religion — and introducing a new theme, incidentally, that I had heard little of in the Holy Land. The theology I had heard there was derived almost wholly from the Bible, but now the Governor began citing Greek philosophy.

"The fourteenth century was the high period of Mount Athos," he said, "because of the movement known as Hesychasm. It was a movement essentially Greek, perhaps going back, in some respects, to Plato. Its aim — which is still the aim of Athonite monasticism — was to see Christ. This can best be done amid quiet and silence — the word *hesychia,* from which Hesychasm is derived, means 'quiet.' There are two worlds — the world of noise and the world of silence — and it is right that those with a passion to hear God's voice should have a silent place, like Mount Athos, to which they can withdraw. Man wants to see the archetype, as Jung says. The Byzantine icon is a window opening into the archetype . . ."

He mentioned the Platonic doctrine of recollection, which he said was important in Athonite thought, and he referred to the theory of forms, as created by poetry. Much of what he said was technical, and I shan't repeat it here, though it was well translated by John Yiannias, who had been studying such matters in both Greek and English. The Governor was lecturing, in effect, and we did not hinder him with questions. We sat listening in his office, which was of whitewashed masonry, with a large desk and a well-stocked bookcase. He was wearing a brown jacket, a multicolored sweater, and gray trousers, and I noticed that he had fine, strong hands. He was clearly well read, and I have since heard that he came from a learned Greek family. He talked on intensely, with pauses for translation, while water trickled in the garden outside his window.

"The recollection of God is arrived at through *askesis*," he said, "— through the ascetic life. Through the doing of Christ-like things, the repetition of holy acts and thoughts. Humility is at the base of it — *askesis* all depends on humility. In monastic life the elders teach the young men, and they always begin by instilling humility in them — instilling absolute obedience." He said much more by the way as well, referring to Dostoevsky, Saint Paul, and Saint Gregory of Nyssa, an Eastern father of the Church.

Then he returned to Hesychasm, and to a fourteenth-century Athonite controversy — still not forgotten there — about monkish visions of the "light on Mount Tabor," where Christ underwent His Transfiguration, according to the New Testament. "Christ is a prototype," the Governor said, "as are Hamlet and Prometheus, and he who contemplates it — who contemplates this uncreated light — goes on forever. But there is a difference between God's 'essence' and his 'energies.' Man can perceive the latter, but not the former . . ."

The Governor talked on, referring to *Pilgrim's Progress*, to Kierkegaard, and to the early Gnostics. Then he spoke of Adam's fall, and the need to recover from it by monastic contemplation. "In short," he finally said, "the goal of monasticism is the achievement by man of a paradisiacal existence."

I felt (with my Asiatic bias) that the Governor was describing much the same thing as Hindu and Buddhist sages talk about, although in other words. I asked if this was so, but he denied it, saying — though I believe not quite correctly — that Asian mystics try to quench the passion for the Divine, while Christian ones encourage it.

He also touched, in answer to another question, on the difference between Eastern and Western Christianity, saying that the former is much influenced by Plato and the latter by Aristotle — he maintained that too much interest in Aristotle has made the West materialistic. Then later he talked of the differences between Christianity and Greek pagan mysticism, but this again was technical.

The interview, or monologue, had now lasted for an hour, and I began asking more down-to-earth questions. The Governor conceded, for one thing, that Mount Athos is in a crisis now, with the monastic population falling off, and with little public zeal for replenishing it. But he maintained that the crisis is but a reflection of one in the outside world, and that Athos will survive it. He felt it was his duty to help in this.

"The Greek State," he said, "has for an objective the preservation of Athonite monasticism. We are doing everything we can to help. We have also, since 1952, done specific work in restoring some of the monasteries' art here, and in building fireproof libraries for some of them." He mentioned a few of these works by name and mentioned certain paintings in the monasteries that we should see, and monks that we should talk with.

"In 1963," he went on, "we are celebrating the thousandth anniversary of Athonite monasticism. This will be done mainly at the monastery of the Great Lavra, which is the oldest on the peninsula. It will be done in true monastic simplicity — there will be a spiritual symposium, for instance, in which Orthodox theologians, philosophers, and others will take part. We are also hoping to attract more visitors to Mount Athos. We don't want tourists here, for tourists and monasticism don't mix, but we will be glad to have more pilgrims and more scholars. We are planning new footpaths in our forests, too. We are not building motor roads on the peninsula — as some laymen have suggested — but we are greatly improving the road from

Salonika to Ouranopolis, near Ierissos. We are building a hotel at Ouranopolis as well, where the wives of our visitors may await them.

"Beyond that we are trying to acquaint all the Orthodox world with Mount Athos, in the hope that more men will become monks. Our one basic law there is freedom, and if you stay long you will see that monks from many nations are living among us, in peace and co-operation. The only requirement is that they must be Orthodox."

We took our leave and went in search of Yohannan, whom we found lunching on bean soup and olives at a nearby monastery, called Koutloumousiou. We joined him, then later we all set out together for a Russian *skete*, Saint Andrew's, which was also in the outskirts of Karyes. Though only a *skete* — a dependency of Vatopedi's — Saint Andrew's is bigger than some of the full-fledged Athonite monasteries. In the nineteenth century, indeed, it sought the rank of monastery, with a voice in running the Holy Community. At that time, one gathers, great numbers of Russian Hesychasts were coming as monks to Athos; the Czarist government — keen to spread its influence — was backing them; and the peninsula was in danger of being overrun.* Saint Andrew's was part of the Russian movement. It was built only in the mid-nineteenth century, and before long it had seven hundred monks in it — living rather splendidly, one hears. Greek countermaneuvers kept it from becoming a monastery, and in time

* This nineteenth-century Russian expansionism was sometimes favorable to Greek Orthodox interests, sometimes opposed to them. In the Church of the Nativity, as I had seen, Russian power had helped the Greeks against the Roman Catholics. But on Athos — otherwise a wholly Greek preserve — it had appeared as a rival.

the Russian Revolution left it stranded — the Russian authorities have tried, in recent years, to send new monks to
Athos, but Greece has refused them, no doubt fearing Red
penetration. Hence the Russian numbers on Athos have
dwindled far more sharply than the Greek, and we had heard
that Saint Andrew's was a leading sufferer.

The *skete* was located five or ten minutes out of town,
by a lane between man-high stone walls. We climbed one
of these en route and viewed our objective from afar. It
seemed an impressive, handsome composition in a style
that might be called Russian baroque — akin to the English Georgian that is so common in our schools and colleges.
It was vast and widespread, with more than a dozen green
onion-domes rising from different parts of it. We drew
closer, and I estimated the near façade at a hundred yards
in length. Behind it — pushing on — we found a stately
assemblage of domes, pediments, columns, arches, and vistas; but all this was sadly deserted now, and on every hand
the courts were growing up to grass and weeds. There had
been a fire in the buildings of one corner, too, and the damage was not repaired. Elsewhere there were broken window-
panes and heavy stillness; and wood was piled roughly by
once elegant doors. A cat crossed a courtyard, silent in the
silence. Then a woodpecker sounded nearby, and the place
seemed lonelier than ever.

In time we found an old monk with a greasy habit and
big Russian boots. He had a red face, blue eyes, and a
whitish-yellow beard, and he seemed morose and uncom-
municative. We passed on and found another, smaller monk
— also dingy and dispirited, but less taciturn. Yohannan
knew some Russian and could talk with him. He said he was
sixty-eight years old, and was the next to youngest in the
monastery — twelve monks lived there altogether, he

added, the oldest being eighty-eight. He went and got a key, and then unlocked the church and showed it to us. It was huge and garish, full of pretentious giltwork and of over-naturalistic icons in the style that we call "candy-box" — the kind of thing we blame, in America, on Victorianism. On the outside Saint Andrew's had seemed impressive — if less attractive than the older Greek monasteries — but here it wasn't even that. Yet the church's interior was well kept up, for all the establishment's general crumbling.

A White Russian in Athens had given Yohannan presents — red cardboard Easter eggs — for a couple of friends, both Russian monks, who lived near Karyes, and it turned out that this old monk at Saint Andrew's knew them, though he said that one of them had died just recently; he had fallen off a cliff, perhaps with the help of *raki*. The monk said the other lived in a *kellion* — a dependency of Saint Andrew's itself — on the hillside not far above us, and we set out to find it. We succeeded, too, though after some hesitation, for the *kellion*'s approach seemed deserted and unpromising. The gate was fastened by a heavy chain and padlock, but some of its wooden bars were out, leaving a hole where one could stoop and go through. We did so, then followed a path in the grass beyond. This took us near a large old, Russian-style house, which looked empty, then to some terraces and arbors, then later past a smaller, secondary building. The ruined garden was lovely — a green carpet in the warm sun, with flies buzzing near by. Wild flowers — pink, yellow, white, and blue — were growing everywhere, too, and birds were singing.

The path went right beside the secondary building, which was locked and lifeless. It was long, with ten or twenty rooms inside it. They had once been the quarters, one imagined, of individual monks, but now they were abandoned, seemingly forever, and left in great disorder. We looked through the windows and saw jumbles of crockery, fallen plaster, old tools, and torn-up books lying round. We went on further, and the path rose a little, and suddenly we came on the dead monk's grave. It had fresh earth over it, and a wooden cross with the monk's name, which Yohannan recognized. The grave looked peaceful in the sunshine, but also makeshift, and the thickets seemed all ready to close in.

The path no longer looked worthwhile, so we turned back toward the main house, and as we did so a Greek laborer appeared — he turned out to be deaf — and beckoned us in that direction. Approaching the house from a new angle now, we saw some signs of life around it — a well-tended garden patch, for one thing, with onions, beets, and lettuce pushing up from the brown earth. Four mallard ducks and a drake came out from near the house, too, looking very familial (one often hears that no female animals are allowed on Athos, but actually female poultry, and cats, are common there).

The deaf laborer took us to a back porch, and then to a small wing or outbuilding, and in this — on opening the door — we found the monk whom we were seeking. He was grayish-blond and bearded, like the monks at Saint Andrew's, but his morale seemed better than theirs — he had clear blue eyes; and his face, rather aquiline, seemed proud and self-respecting. He was living in a corner of the wing — camping there, one might say. He was the last survivor of what must have been a large community — dozens of monks — and in his isolation he had shortened his perimeter, in the military phrase.

His small domain — in what might once have been a pantry — was neat, too, if not meticulously clean. He had a bed there, and some books and furniture and utensils. With the help of the deaf Greek — who seemed to work for him, at least part-time — he made some Turkish coffee for us on a spirit lamp. He seemed delighted with the Easter eggs, and thankful for news of his friend in Athens, and he told Yohannan at length about the other monk's death. He seemed in good spirits, yet in those surroundings one reflected, inevitably, that he too would die some day, and one wondered who would tell of that.

This *kellion* was the last Russian place we visited on Athos. There is a Russian monastery on the peninsula — one of the twenty — and John Yiannias and I passed it a few days later, in a caïque. It was a huge affair, rather like Saint Andrew's in style, but more barracks-like — its larger buildings recalled the great, monotonous chunks of housing that the Soviets are building in Russia today. I have read that the monastery contains thirty churches and chapels, and that it housed fifteen hundred monks in its heyday, but that now it is down to a score or so.

In addition Mount Athos has some four or five other Russian *sketae,* a Bulgarian monastery, a Bulgarian *skete,* two Rumanian *sketae,* and many Russian or other Slavic *kellia.* These have had no — or virtually no — reinforcements from their own countries since the Second World War. Of the non-Greek monasteries only Chilandari, the Serbian one, which draws from Yugoslavia, has had new monks, and those not many. The Slavic world used to play a lively part on Athos — I have read, incidentally, that Rasputin was a frequent visitor — but that phase seems nearly ended.

We left Karyes in the afternoon. The next objective, for Yiannias and myself, was the Great Lavra, more simply called just Lavra (the word means a "street of cells"). It was far away — just north of the peninsula's eastern tip — and we didn't expect to reach it till the following afternoon, going by a jitney caïque that was due to sail at midday from Daphni, the Athonite seaport. Daphni, in turn, was on the south coast, a few miles distant from Karyes — over the peninsula's spine — and we planned to reach there in the morning, after sleeping at an intervening monastery, called Xeropotamou. Our task now was to make Xeropotamou, therefore, and to make it by sunset, when the gate would close.

This closing of the gates is a main feature of life on Athos, and it had a good reason in the past. In the Middle Ages the peninsula was raided again and again by pirates and other marauders — Turks, Arabs, and West European "Crusaders." * Safety lay only in fortification, and this has governed the design of all but the newest monasteries. The older ones have inner courtyards, where stand the church and other key institutions; they have their high towers, or keeps, designed as last resorts; and they have massive armor-plated gates. In the old days these gates were closed at sunset against night attack, and now they are still closed then because of tradition, which is so strong on Athos. Hence sunset is a crucial moment in one's calculations. In eighteen of the twenty monasteries, furthermore, that moment is called twelve o'clock, for such was the Byzantine custom; and the monastic timepieces are forever being re-set — to their detriment, one hears — as the days grow longer or shorter. The two exceptions to this

* Sometimes "Crusaders," claiming allegiance to the Pope, used to set up as robber barons on the Greek mainland, and from there they would raid the Athonite monasteries when the spirit moved them. This was one more reason, of course, for bad feeling between the Eastern and Western Churches.

rule are Vatopedi, an innovator that uses our Western time-system, and Iviron, which uses the old Chaldean one, whereby not sunset, but sunrise, is counted as twelve. (Vatopedi also, alone of the Athonite monasteries, uses the modern, Gregorian calendar instead of the Julian.) During our stay on Athos one monk quoted Scripture — characteristically — to explain why the Byzantine time-system is the right one: in the Gospel account of the Crucifixion, he pointed out, it is recorded that darkness fell between the sixth and ninth hours, a statement that would be meaningless if dark had been expected then anyway.*

While we were on Athos the sun was setting around seven, and we left Karyes that afternoon at four, which gave us lots of time. Yohannan was still with us, and planned to take the caïque part way toward Lavra. We had engaged a mule to carry our things to Xeropotamou, but it didn't show up, so we carried them ourselves. The road again was of stone, and for half an hour it zig-zagged steeply up the hillside — we kept getting higher and higher views down onto the capital, which continued to seem a charming hamlet in the greenness. In time we made the ridgeline — there was a shrine there, under a chestnut tree — and then dropped down to Xeropotamou, reaching it early enough to relax, in the late sunlight, on a balcony. The monastery was on a broad bench high above the southern coast. Out below our balcony were many garden patches, chocolate-brown in color, with jade-green vegetables. Beyond them was a mass of silvery olive trees, and over their tops we looked down on the sea itself, which was calm and blue that afternoon.

* I am told that the custom of resetting clocks at sunrise and/or sunset is even pre-Byzantine, having existed among the ancient Jews (and being still in force, moreover, among the Arabs "of old mentality").

We had a delicious lentil soup for dinner, and the guest-master even slipped us some olive-oil to put in it (because, he said, we were "growing boys"). We had a good sleep, too, but a wind came up in the night, and we could hear its buffeting outside. In the morning the sea had white-caps on it, and this raised a question about our trip, for the headland of Mount Athos — the Persians' nemesis, which a boat must round between Daphni and Lavra — is dangerous in rough weather. We meant to get as far as we could, however, so we walked to Daphni anyway, as we had planned — going down a stone road and along the shore a ways, and reaching there about ten.

As Karyes is the Washington of Athos, so Daphni is its New York — its major port, through which flows most of its traffic with the *cosmos,* the outside world. The place consists of a jetty, a sea-wall, a stone esplanade, and a row of white-washed buildings, three of which house stores and one a restaurant. The restaurant has an arbor out in front, and today this was wholly covered by wistaria in bloom. Today the esplanade looked busy, too, in a quiet way, with laymen, monks, and mules in motion or standing around. Two or three caïques lay at the jetty, and we learned that one would start for Lavra all right, though it might turn back en route after dropping its passengers. We didn't mind risking that — we felt pretty sure of a lodging along the way — so we settled down to wait for the hour or two before the boat would leave.

Commercially Daphni is like many frontier settlements — like a trading-post in Africa, for instance. Its shops stock food such as canned sardines, evaporated milk, dried figs, and even a few fresh oranges and lemons. They stock flash-lights, bolts of cloth, and bottled liqueurs. Also flit-guns, bags of cement, and rolls of tin sheeting; and out in front of them stand fifty-gallon gasoline drums. These things are displayed in a practical, non-fancy, rather fly-specked way; and that day the monks and laymen were coming and going among them; sometimes old friends — a couple of hermits, perhaps — would meet and greet enthusiastically, as in reunions in a mining country.

When the caïque was ready, a great many passengers got aboard. Most were monks — several returning for Easter, apparently, to their home stations from Karyes or Daphni. Easter was in the air, in fact, though it was still but Tuesday; and farewell shouts of *"Kalo Pascha"* — "Happy Easter" — flew between caïque and shore as we pulled away. The atmosphere on the boat was friendly. The cabin was just high enough so that on either side one could half-sit, half-lean against it with one's feet on the gunwhale; and two lines of passengers formed up now doing this, both looking outward with the baggage in behind — between us — on the cabin's top.

I had got a position on the port or landward side, where I could watch the peninsula as we went along. Again it was green and hilly, but somewhat drier-looking than the north side had been. The peak of Athos itself was nearer now, and would grow still more so as the day wore on. It was of bare, jagged gray rock — snow-streaked — above the green foothills. I have read that the rock is marble, though I am not sure of this. The green hills near us had cliffs on them now and then, and a cover of what looked like scrub-oak. Sometimes olive groves — hanging on the steepness — would take the place of this. Once we passed a long white torrent falling from a cliff. We saw a trail along the land-face, too, and once or twice we saw a bent monkish figure walking on it, with stick and knapsack.

We passed four monasteries in the next hour or two,

among which one, called Simonos **Petra**, is perhaps the most spectacular of all on Athos. It stands high on the hillside, built straight up, like a bundle of shafts, on a base of rocky pinnacles. It has balcony over balcony across its tall, bleak façades; and it too — like so many things on Athos — reminded me of monasteries in Tibet. Later I went up there — on the way back from Lavra — but I almost regretted having done so, for the monastery is new, and there is little in it of distinction. I got a fine sense of space when standing on its balconies, but otherwise I had enjoyed it more from down below. At that later time I also visited the three other monasteries in this region; and with John Yiannias was in one of them, called Dionysiou, when Easter came. But now we merely saw the four from down on the water. They all had the common traits of Athonite monasteries — the impregnable walls, the balconies staring into the void, and so on.

They also all had landings, at each of which we stopped, and at one of which we dropped Yohannan. Monks got on and off at the landings too, and so did packages. These latter were handed back and forth, to be relayed to their destinations by a system that I didn't fathom, but that seemed to work. The Greek postal service extends to Athos, I had learned, but only to Karyes and Daphni, beyond which mail is on its own. Sometimes it is forwarded, apparently, by the Karyes delegates of the monasteries, and sometimes it is just passed along. People know each other's business on Athos, it seems, and they are co-operative, and the things move on somehow.

I had made a friend by now on the caïque, a little old monk who spoke some English and who said he had lived in America early in the century — working, for a few years,

with the General Electric Company in Lynn, Massachusetts.
After that he had come back to Greece and come straight
to Athos. His case was not unique, either, I was to learn —
in the next few days I met half a dozen monks who had
lived in America. This one's name was Timotheos, and he
had blue eyes, wispy gray hair, a thin face, and an insub-
stantial-looking body. He was altogether meek and mild,
and friendly, and he seemed extremely happy. He said he
lived in a *kellion* at a place named Kapsokalyvia, out near
the point toward Lavra, and that he and two other monks
there supported themselves by carving wooden icons and
souvenirs. He had a big, heavy goat-hair bag with him, and
before long he dipped into it and brought out two wooden
paper-cutters and two pairs of wooden tongs — for fruit,
perhaps — that he insisted on giving to John Yiannias and
myself. He would take nothing in return — he seemed to
enjoy the giving.

We left the region of the four monasteries, and soon we
came to settlements of another kind — to more random
sketae and *kellia* on the hillside. *Sketae* on Athos are of
two kinds: some are unified, like Saint Andrew's, and some
are disjointed, with little buildings scattered in the neighborhood of a central church. These *sketae* now were of the
latter sort, with many houses plastered about on the steep,
high slopes. We were rounding a southward bulge near
Athos's tip by this time. The peak was above us, and the
land was apparently sheltered from heavy cold and rainfall
— we even saw cactuses growing there. We ourselves were
sheltered from the wind now, too. The sun was warm, the
sky was blue, and the water clear. I took to lying back on
the cabin — feeling the boat throb under me, listening to
the monks talk, and looking at the *sketae* and *kellia* over-

head, which were getting to be more and more like swallows' nests against the cliffs.

We rounded a minor point and came underneath some cliffs known as Karoulia — "The Pulleys." There was a jetty there, with steps going up from it like a ladder; and then dotted on the cliffs were façades of what might be called small houses, except that there was plainly little behind them but caves. They could be reached, we saw, by vertical step-ways and horizontal shelves. That view was the only one we had of Karoulia on our trip, but I have since learned it is a main area for hermits on Mount Athos. (Its name comes from pulleys that are used to raise supplies, or lower them, to the caves there.)

We rounded a second minor point and met the wind, and soon the caïque was tossing sharply. "We've begun the dance," one monk said, according to Yiannias. No one seemed to mind it, though — the monks were laughing and smiling, while their beards and hair were blowing in the breeze. But the captain gave up on Lavra. He said he would turn back at the next stop, which was Kapsokalyvia, the home of Father Timotheos.

The landing there was in a little cove, like a smuggler's cove in John Masefield, with steps going up the cliff. The boat tossed wildly by the jetty, but the monks swarmed nimbly off it, carrying their baggage and that of others, too — everyone helping everyone else. Then we had a steep climb for ten or fifteen minutes, and after that we were in the settlement itself, a colony of little houses on a hillside that recalled the Riviera — or the Big Sur in California — with the dryness of its scrub and the blueness of the sea it looked out over. The sea ran on and on away from us — blue as could be — till it vanished in a cool mist off toward Asia.

At the *skete* of Kapsokalyvia we had jam and *raki* on a sunny terrace, but we didn't linger there, for it turned out we could try for Lavra that same day. A returning monk of Lavra, accompanied by a student, had happened to be on our caïque, and so had a Greek policeman bound for there. Now, as we sat on the terrace, the monk — also taking some refreshment — explained that the road to Lavra, across the point, would take a little more than two hours of fast walking. We could do it before darkness fell, he said, if we used baggage mules, and there happened to be two available at Kapsokalyvia. So we all, including the policeman, clubbed together in the project. It was almost five o'clock, and there seemed but little chance of making Lavra by the deadline; but still we two were in good company now, and we didn't worry.

Father Timotheos appeared, and, while the mules were being loaded, he took John Yiannias and me ahead to see his *kellion* — it was across a ravine and just downhill from the Lavra path. It turned out to be a pleasant little cottage with a garden and a tiny chapel — all *kellia* have chapels of their own, I gathered. We met another old monk there who had also worked for the General Electric in Lynn, Massachusetts — he was the "elder" of the *kellion,* and Timotheos was his disciple, though the latter's age, he had told us, was eighty-one. They fed us more jam and *raki,* and showed us pocket icons — reliefs on bits of wood — that they had carved. We each bought a couple, though there was no salesmanship involved — Timotheos would be happy if we bought them, it seemed, and equally happy if we didn't. He gave an extraordinary impression of bliss and innocence. "On the caïque," John Yiannias told me later, "Timotheos was describing how Mount Athos is the 'garden of the Virgin Mary.' He seemed transported with

rapture while he talked about it." That was just like
Timotheos.

We didn't stay long at the *kellion,* but scrambled up the
hillside to the Lavra path, and soon the others came along
with the mules. John Yiannias and the monk — his name
was Father Elias — rode from time to time thereafter,
while the others of us walked. I was in fair shape for walking — having done a good deal of it in the past month or
two — but the policeman, who led us, set a fearful pace.
The path went round gorges and across the face of bluffs
— one of the latter was wholly covered by a recent ava-
lanche. The sea was always in view — below us and to the
right — all darkening and wrinkled. The policeman kept
his pistol drawn theatrically as he walked — the wolves
were bad on Athos, he maintained — and meanwhile he
hurried over the rocks as if in seven-league boots (the
mules, thank Heaven, were slower, and we halted now and
then to wait for them).

At length we reached a pass — a shoulder — and turned
downward to the left, and after that began glimpsing Lavra
in the distance. It was vast, and of dim masonry, with tall
black cypresses beside it. The path was bigger now — it had
become a first-class Athonite stone road — and we went
swiftly down it after the policeman. Then suddenly he disappeared — he merely put on speed and left us. He was
going ahead, it later developed, to keep the gate from
closing. He made it, too, and when darkness fell we all were
safe inside.

We spent two nights and a day at Lavra, and the place
was like something from the *Idylls of the King.* It gave me
that feeling when we approached it, in the evening, and
gave it more strongly still the next day, when I took a walk

outside. To the gate's right lay an expanse of pebble-mosaic on the ground, then came a belvedere, then olive groves running down to the sea. I turned left, though, around the monastery's end — passing some old stone out-buildings, with irrigation water babbling through them — then went on to the vineyards, orchards, and gardens of the monks, which were mainly on some flat ground to the southeast. Old stone walls were there, and wooden gates with crosses on their tops. The vegetables were growing in small plots, and they included, at that season, beans, onions, carrots, lettuce, spinach, and — off to the side — big arti-chokes. I saw some monks, but many more laymen, work-ing in the gardens. The whole area was overlooked by the high, and very long, monastery wall. This was of old stone — brownish-gray in color, rough in texture — going up to weathered frame balconies above. There were earth smells in the gardens, too, and compost heaps about.

The court inside the monastery was long — almost like a block-long street — with the church, refectory, and other buildings standing in it, and with living quarters all around it; these had odd little balconies and outside stairways. There were fruit trees, too, just coming into leaf and bloom, and two huge cypresses that were said — I don't know how seriously — to have been planted in the tenth century. The main church — *catholicon* is the technical term — was maroon, like several others we saw on Athos, and near it, against a wall, were some ochre benches where one could sit in the sun. Despite these the court had less color than Vatopedi's, but it had a more attractive feeling of age. The tower or keep was said to date from the tenth century, and it looked it. A great marble bowl in the court, for holy water, went back to that time too. Yet these things didn't have a monumental, self-important look; they seemed primarily, rather, to be well-worn and livable. The courtyard was informal. Mules came into it that day, and wandered round; cats sunned themselves in it; and yellow jackets buzzed away there.

Father Elias turned out to be a scholar, and well informed. He spent much of the day with us, conversing in the courtyard (his duties as host relieving him, perhaps, of onerous Holy Week vigils). I also read a certain amount about Lavra. It is the oldest monastery on Athos — founded in 963 — and also the senior in prestige. It was founded by a Byzantine monk — later called Saint Athanasius — who was helped in the task by two Byzantine emperors. There had been hermits on Mount Athos for an unknown length of time before that — living in imitation of Saint Anthony and the other Desert holy men of Egypt and Palestine — but Athanasius thought the religious life there needed discipline. He conceived the Great Lavra accordingly — also in imitation, of Middle Eastern establishments like Mar Saba — and the idea must have taken hold at once, for at least four other Athonite monasteries, including Vatopedi and Iviron, were likewise founded in the tenth century. More followed in the centuries just after that, and Mount Athos got much support from Byzantine rulers and courtiers — also from nobles among the newly converted Slavs. It became, to a large degree, the spiritual center of Orthodoxy in the centuries when the Eastern Church was splitting from the Western.

In 1453 Constantinople fell to the Moslem Turks, but this was less of a blow to Athos than it might have been, for the Turkish policy was lenient. The peninsula kept much of its autonomy right down to the Greek War of Independence, in the early nineteenth century. But then the monks openly helped their countrymen, and in reprisal Turkish troops moved onto Athos — occupying it, doing damage, and causing many monks to leave. One trace of their presence could still be seen at Lavra — they had scratched the eyes out of many figures in religious murals there (which they had looked on, in the Moslem way, as idolatrous).

Even though the Turks left Athos alone, at first, their victory put an end to the old court patronage, and in time this caused some monasteries, including Lavra, to change their inner structure. They switched from the old centralized rule — called "cenobitic" — to an improvised one called "idiorrhythmic," under which monks were told to help pay their own expenses, to keep their own gardens, to make their own wine and so on, in return for being kept under less strict discipline and being allowed to prepare meals in their own quarters. The innovation stuck, and of the twenty Athonite monasteries nine are idiorrhythmic today. We learned from Father Elias, however, that the idiorrhythmic system is being much criticized, as promoting a slackness ill-suited to the trials now facing the Athonite community. He said he thought Lavra should mark its thousandth year by returning to cenobitic rule, which it could well afford because of its timber sales.

The paintings at Lavra are rated among the best on Athos, and we had a good chance to see them. They were in the main church — *catholicon* — and the refectory, covering the walls of both. Their purpose, like that of most Byzantine art, was to edify their viewers in religion, and they had been placed with this in mind. The refectory at Lavra is used now only on state occasions, because of the idiorrhythmic system, but when the place was cenobitic its monks were exposed to the murals at every meal — monks are still exposed to murals, in fact, in the cenobitic monasteries on Athos that have them. There is no table-talk in these cenobitic refectories. Instead there is religious reading by a monk, who stands in a sort of pulpit; and for the eyes there is a feast of paintings (the purpose of art in the Athonite *catholica* is yet more obvious to a visitor, for it is parallel to Western Church usage).

In earlier times the movement called iconoclasm almost did away with Byzantine religious art, on the grounds of idolatry, but it lost out in the ninth century, before Lavra was even thought of, and since then icons — "images" or "pictures" — have been part of the standard apparatus for teaching the faith. (The existing murals at Lavra, however, date from only the sixteenth century.)

Lavra's refectory was open all day long while we were there, and we could drop in as we chose. The *catholicon* was locked, but Father Elias got a key and showed us around it. The murals in both places were much alike. They were painted on plaster — as frescoes, I think — and in color they leaned to blacks and reds. Those in the refectory were disposed in three bands, or levels, across the broad high walls. The top level concerned the life of Christ, and events related to it. The second concerned the lives of martyrs — or more strictly their deaths, often gruesomely portrayed. The bottom one held stylized portraits of ascetics, including several Athonite saints — among them Athanasius, Lavra's founder. Monks eating — or fasting — in the refectory could be heartened by these examples. There were also some special items in the buildings — a painting of the Last Supper, notably, above the abbot's table at the end.

In the *catholicon* the murals dealt more purely with the life of Christ. Lavra's *catholicon* was shaped almost exactly like those at Vatopedi and Iviron, and indeed like nearly all the ones on Athos. Its small nave was nearly square in floor-plan, the sides rising up and up to narrow, lofty arches, these leading farther upward to a dome. All the inner surfaces had pictures on them. In the dome, as always, was the Byzantine version of Christ as Pantocrator, and below it, in set positions, were other standard scenes: the Crucifixion, the Resurrection, and so on.

Among the most highly placed was a picture of the Transfiguration on Mount Tabor, an event that the Governor had mentioned to us and that really was — according to my reading — an all-important subject in Athonite thought. According to the Gospel story — and the painting in Lavra's *catholicon* — Christ was transfused on that occasion by a mysterious light, which was visible to a few of His disciples. Long afterward the Hesychasts of Athos maintained that this light was an objective, permanent, ubiquitous Divine reality, which holy men could apprehend in an extrasensory way. To do this was the goal of the Hesychasts' monasticism, insofar as they were serious mystics. Then their belief was challenged, in the fourteenth century, by a Humanist element in Constantinople — influenced by the budding Renaissance of Italy — which maintained that nothing could be apprehended extrasensorily. A great controversy arose; the Hesychast position was well upheld by a Lavra monk, later known as Saint Gregory Palamas; and in the end the Orthodox Church authorities declared for it.

In time Humanism swept through Western Europe, as we know, but Athos kept aloof from it, and has done so ever since — and that, so far as I have learned, is the main difference between the Athonite philosophy and our own.*

* In its theological heat this controversy — over "the light on Mount Tabor" — seems to have been much like the early Christian ones —

Some murals in the *catholicon* had been cleaned and re-
stored, and these were more brilliant, and easier to see, than
the others, which had suffered, after all, from four centuries of candle-smoke and other exhalations. The cleaning had been halted, though, and Father Elias said the
monastery was going slow with it — those in charge were
pleased with the results so far, but were on guard against
bad aftereffects. The Greek authorities were helping in the
work, as the Governor in Karyes had said. In fact the murals at Lavra and some other monasteries — and in the
Protaton, the old church at Karyes — are now being looked
on as masterpieces of Christian art, no longer to be left to
the care of inexperienced monks. For a long time Byzantine
art was frowned on by the world at large, as not up to classi-
cal or Renaissance standards. Now, though, the tendency
is to judge it by standards of its own, as an art that seeks
not to catch earthly beauty, but to convey spiritual mean-
ings impressionistically and subjectively — by primitive
techniques with strong feeling behind them.

Seen in this way, the paintings at Lavra were forceful.
The figures were conventionalized in their dress. John the
Baptist, for instance, always had olive-brown clothes draped
round him. His hair was long, with conventional tangles
in it, and his sandals were tenuous — mere cords bound
round his feet. His face was thin and furrowed, and brown
as a berry — he was the very picture of a desert ascetic, as
John Yiannias said. Other figures were likewise stylized.

Nestorian, Monophysite, etc. — over Christ's nature. But the Athonite
issue is perhaps more easily grasped than the others by a modern man,
for it still exists, if latently, today. It is the issue between the idealist or
transcendentalist philosophy, which believes in a reality that can be felt
only by extrasensory means — by intuition or inspiration — and the Ma-
terialist, which holds that "nothing comes to us except through the five
senses."

They could almost be called cartoons, except that they had great color in them and great depth of feeling. And one met them again and again, not just at Lavra, but at other monasteries, too, and always done in much the same way, so that the effect was cumulative — John the Baptist became a figure one cared about. Many of the other stock characterizations were moving, too — the Byzantine Christ, for instance, seemed to grow on one more subtly than do the Italian Christs, which for all their beauty have, perhaps, less strength.

Lavra held many other things to look at, for it is the richest of the Athonite monasteries in nearly all ways. Apart from the murals we saw fine old panel icons — small and portable — there. We saw two Bibles, bound in gold with precious stones, that weighed sixty and forty pounds respectively. We saw vestments in a host of bright colors, embroidered with gold thread and jewels — some had saintly figures on them whose halos were all made from little pearls. We saw censers, too, and staffs and chalices, that really should be classed as jewelry. And in the library we saw a fourth-century copy of Saint Paul's Epistle to the Galatians — said to be the oldest document on Athos — along with many other manuscripts, and illuminations, and samples of Byzantine musical notation.

In between seeing those sights, and talking with the monks, we passed the time in our quarters. The guestmaster at Lavra — a smallish, obliging, personable monk named Zacharias — took special pains with his cuisine. On our first evening he gave us a fine pea soup, and on our second a lavish spread of beans, green onions, noodles, olives, and boiled potatoes. We had company in the guest quarters, too, including the German boy scout we had met at Vatopedi, a score of Greek schoolboys on vacation, and

a charming Englishman who belonged to the Orthodox
Church — he made frequent trips to Athos, he told us, and
by good luck he would travel with us on the next stage of
our journey.

We were supposed to get mules from Lavra, but again
they didn't show up, thanks to Easter. The Athonite monasteries' mules are in the charge of laymen, as a rule, and
an exodus of laymen was on — many had families at Ierissos
or elsewhere, and they were off to join them for the holiday.
We might have waited at Lavra for a caïque, but we knew
that the waters off the headland were uncertain, and we
didn't care to go back along the north coast to Iviron and
Karyes, another alternative. We wanted to cross the headland to the south again, so when the mules didn't come we
picked up our bags and started walking; there were three of
us now, with the Englishman out in front — he had a big
knapsack, and he set a slow but steady pace.

We went back up to the pass we had crossed two eve-
nings earlier, and there, while resting, we were overtaken
by a couple of laymen with a mule. They let us put our
things, too, on the mule's back, and after that we walked
unencumbered till midday, when our paths diverged again.
Throughout this time our route lay across the lower slopes
of Mount Athos itself, inland and above the way we had
come by. We didn't even see Kapsokalyvia, where the boat
had dropped us; we saw only hillsides running down in
that direction.

The landscape we passed was like that of low mountain
slopes in many countries — it might have been in the
Himalayan foothills, or those of the Rockies. It had pas-
tures, brush, and cut-off woodland in it, as well as big bare
rocks and snow-fed brooks. The weather was sunny and

cool, ideal for walking — we had had good weather for all our trip so far. The sky was blue above us, and Mount Athos, always looming to our right, was gray and glistening, with here and there a dazzling piece of snow.

The Englishman had climbed the peak a number of times, and he told us about it. The round trip took a day, he said; one could do it from Lavra in a pinch, but it was better to use a nearer base if possible. He seemed to love the scenery. He had a camera with some close-up lenses, and he kept stopping to take pictures of wildflowers, though with Athonite modesty he never admitted to knowing their names. "I think it's a sort of vetch," he would say when questioned; or "I think it's sort of periwinkle kind of thing"; or even "I don't know what it is, but it's delicious." Then he would put his camera six inches from the flower and snap it, in full color. He said that back in England he flashed these intimate pictures on a giant screen, with startling effects.

At noon the mule went its separate way — the laymen turned downhill, to a *skete* in that neighborhood, where they planned to lunch and rest. We others shouldered our bags again, kept to the same level and pushed on, stopping soon for lunch beneath some trees. Zacharias had given us bread and olives, and to this we added dried fruit and chocolate from our knapsacks. The chocolate was donated by the Englishman, who had bought it in Switzerland on his way through there — it was bitter Lindt, and excellent.

Throughout the morning we had seen few dwellings, even in the distance. At noon we had passed a nearly abandoned Russian *skete* — downhill from us — with pretty little *kellia* in desuetude. Now, as we went on after lunch, we began descending, and soon we reached the upper fringe of the hermit region whose bottom we had seen already —

considerably lower — on the cliffs around Karoulia (The Pulleys). Our path went near some hermitages, but we saw few signs of life there. In theory, as I had learned, the monks in that region live like the early Christian hermits and pillar-saints. The best of them are said to be self-effacing, even shy, and to subsist on things like herb soup and stale bread. We passed one hermit's shelter that was empty, and we looked inside it. The place was small and nearly square, with rough stone walls and a roof of corrugated iron sheets, laid loosely on. It had a couch of leafy branches in it, and a stone shelf or two, and that was all.

We were going steeply downward now, through brush on a dry rocky path, and the sun was hot. John Yiannias and I felt we had walked enough that day, and we were heading for a place where we could spend the night — a small establishment of monks who were also icon-painters. The Englishman knew the way there, luckily, and guided us. We reached it in mid-afternoon, and there he left us, after jam and *raki*.

The painters' place was on another terraced bluffside — warm now in the afternoon, with the sea below it reflecting the sun. There were the usual vineyards, gardens, and olive groves nearby — wherever flat ground had been found or made — and the monks had fixed their house up well. Spending-money came into their lives inevitably, for they did a mail-order business in icons, selling them as far away as America. They also seemed industrious — when we were there two of them were repainting an inside hall, for Easter, and others were working on the grounds. There were nine monks altogether, from old men down to youths. The place was organized, we gathered, on the standard Athonite system of elder and disciples. As a rule an Athonite *kellion* houses at least three members

— an elder (or *geron*), a monk in his prime, and a novice. The elder gives spiritual guidance to the others, and later they grow old, and replace him, taking in new members in their turn. Elders are thought vital in Athonite monasticism, rather as *gurus* are among the Hindus. The system is also akin to the master-apprentice relationship of medieval artisans, and in this case it seemed most harmonious, with the older monks teaching the younger while they worked and prayed together.

The present elder, well over eighty, was more or less retired, but we had a talk with the next in line, a monk whose beard was white and whose eyes were black and piercing. The place is known out in the *cosmos,* he told us, as the Iconographic House of the Monk Daniel, one Daniel having been its founder. It has been selling icons for decades now, to Greece, America, and other countries. These have been in two styles — the old Byzantine one and the newer one that I have called "candy-box," and that on Athos is often known as "Russian." The old monk said that he and his colleagues prefer to work in the Byzantine style, but that heretofore the demand has been mainly for the Russian, and so they have gone along. Now things are changing, though, he added; the Byzantine is growing popular again, and even churches in Greece are asking for it, which is a milestone. The house had done icons for several churches in America — including, in fact, the one to which John Yiannias belongs, in Dubuque, Iowa. During our visit the monks were making a Byzantine set of icons, too, for a church in Pittsburgh; and other customers include Greek churches in Kansas and Florida.

Most of the monks' work on hand was upstairs in their chapel and main studio, and they took us up and showed us around there. They seemed to work ably in both styles, but to a man seemed keener on the Byzantine. One young monk told us of experiments they were making in the old techniques — trying to relearn the secrets of tempera and frescoing. Of course they had fine models to work from. Sometimes they borrowed panel icons from the monasteries, the young monk said, and sometimes they went on trips to study neighboring murals. I got the impression that they did not copy slavishly, in the Byzantine style at least, but tried to follow the old masters creatively — I felt, indeed, that they were very much in the old spirit.

The monks' artistic atmosphere extended to their kitchen, and luckily it was Maundy Thursday, when certain leniencies are allowed on Athos, against the heavy fasting of Good Friday. We were allowed wine, and it was good *kokinelli* — a rosé with resin flavoring, which the Greeks go in for. We also had a tasty octopus soup (octopus ranks as neither fish nor meat on Athos, by some quirk of nature — perhaps the same quirk that lets oysters appear in *Lohan tsai,* the Chinese Buddhist vegetarian dish). At the meal's end we had a tasty compote, too, and along the way we had olives, fresh bread, and the Greek sweet known as *halvah*. I can't say what herbs and spices the monks used, but the soup and compote would have been outstanding anywhere. We had the meal in a jolly atmosphere, too — sitting at a long table with the monks themselves.

That night we went to their church service for a while. (On all these nights of Holy Week there had been seven-hour vigils everywhere on Athos, with all the monks taking part, theoretically; John Yiannias had taken part to some degree as well, but I had slept.) This night the service, for which some nearby hermits had come in, was intimate and pleasant, with candlelight in the small chapel, and with antiphonal singing by the handful of monks. We stayed for an hour, then withdrew downstairs to the parlor or reception room, where beds had been made for us on benches.

On Good Friday we reached the monastery of Dionysiou, where we remained till Easter — till leaving Athos, in fact — except for a walk I took, on the Saturday, to some other monasteries nearby. The weather was cloudy now, but the walking was lovely, on a path that went up and down on bluffs by the sea. There were many wildflowers out, among them blue and yellow iris. Mules, too, were grazing in the brush by the path — let loose, no doubt, for the holiday. And at times the water had strange little wind-patterns on it, made by gusts coming down off the peak.

The monasteries I visited did not happen to be outstanding in the museum sense, and anyway I couldn't learn much about them without John Yiannias, who had stayed behind for the important services at Dionysiou. But I did have a look around them, and partook of their hospitality, and in each I chanced to find a monk who had been to America. All told, I met seven such monks on Athos, and except for one of them, at Dionysiou itself, they had been there only briefly, and before the First World War — the early nineteen hundreds were a great time of Greek migration to the States. They had all been youths then. They had worked for a few years in restaurants, on railways, or in factories, and then had come back, and often straight to Athos. If there was any deep significance in this progression — America to Athos — I didn't grasp it. All I found was that the monks were friendly, and well disposed to our country. God bless America, they said in effect, and one of them said it in words.*

The monk at Dionysiou had been in the States much longer than the others. He had become a successful confectioner in Atlanta, Georgia, and he said he had crossed the Atlantic sixteen times. In fact he had decorated his cell in a way to suggest a cabin on the *Queen Mary* — its windows looked right out to sea, over a narrow balcony that might have been a deck. The monk's name was Father Hilarion. He was a small man, alert and vigorous, and he read the liturgy a good deal in the church. He was cheerful company. He made coffee in his room once for John Yiannias and me, and gave us other refreshments. "Would you like some fruit?" he said then. "I have some oranges and bananas here." He paused. "Yes, we have no bananas," he said. "That was a song in the U.S., you know." Then he sang a little of it. "Yes, we have no bananas," he sang. "We have no bananas today." He had an iron-gray beard and a Napoleonic little figure, and in his English the Greek and Dixie accents strove against each other.

He said he had come to Athos in 1937 — he had been married just before that, but his wife had died, and he had evidently felt that worldly ties were not for him. I asked him why he had chosen Dionysiou, which is cenobitic, and reputed very strict, instead of some idiorrhythmic monastery, where he would certainly have been welcome and could have lived more comfortably. "I might as well have stayed in the U.S. as do that," he answered. He named a well-known idiorrhythmic monastery on Athos. "They

---

* America and Athos have both been escapes from modern Greek life, which has been hard for many poor people. If a young Greek did badly in America, he might find in Athos a second way out. And then in time, perhaps, he might forget the harshness of his immigrant days here.

have everything there," he said, "but that's not what I came here for. I want to be near God." Yet he confessed to having a sweet tooth, and said he took the jitney caïque to Daphni once or twice a month and bought candy there.

Where present conduct is concerned, Dionysiou has the best name, perhaps, of all the Athonite monasteries. In Greece one hears the standard anti-clerical charges made about the monks on Athos — they are accused of parasitism, escapism, misogyny, unnatural vice, and so on. Each of these charges seems to be true in some cases, and in our trip we often met monks who seemed altogether worldly. But at Dionysiou such faults seemed at a minimum. Most monks there gave the impression of being serious, and of really keeping the fasts and vigils — some of them were plainly quite fatigued by Easter. There were at least two well-known theologians, too, at Dionysiou. One was the abbot himself, a strong man with kindly eyes, a big beard, and a handshake like a vice. The other was a Father Theokletos, a younger man — a monk for twenty years now — who was plainly an aesthete or intellectual; he had a thin, pale face, with a long nose, a long black beard, and deep, dark eyes. We saw little of the abbot, for he was called away during part of our visit, to the funeral of a colleague in another monastery. But we did have two long talks with Father Theokletos, and I also read some excerpts from his writings — he has written a lot, though little has been translated from the Greek.

We talked in his cell, which was near that of Father Hilarion, the ex-confectioner. It was a simple, primitive room with plaster walls — the walls weren't even truly square or straight. It had a board bed with a rug on it, two crude wooden tables, two chairs, a few icons, and a bookcase overflowing with books and pamphlets. One of our talks was in the evening, and the room was lit by a little kerosene lamp — through the dark windows we could hear the wind, and hear the waves beating on the rocks below.

Mount Athos was chiefly significant, the Father said, as an example of Biblical and Orthodox Christianity being lived as it should be. "The perfect Christian life can only be led away from the world," he said, "and fleeing to the wilderness follows naturally on that fact." Then he mentioned the importance of tradition in Athonite practice — he talked about the "continuous renewal of the very same experience" as the first Church Fathers had had. "Athos," he said, "continues the tradition of the Fathers spiritually and historically. And in order to interpret Athos, one must see it through this lens of tradition." Later in his writings I found this statement too: "Without monasticism religion couldn't exist, for monasticism constitutes its aristocracy, its zealots, those dedicated to it." *

In the writings of Theokletos I found great praise for the hermit's life, so I asked him why there should be monasteries at all on Athos. "Why not just have hermits?" I

---

* I have also read, elsewhere, that Orthodox monks see themselves as descended spiritually from the prophets of Israel, who often lived apart in the Jordan Valley or the Judean Wilderness — the descent is said to have passed from the prophets through John the Baptist and Saint Paul to the ascetic Church Fathers like Saint Anthony. In this view, the Orthodox one, the parentage of Christian monasticism is thus confined entirely to Biblical figures. Yet with the unorthodox (at least with me) the suspicion still dies hard that farther Eastern influences — and also the Qumran monastery of the Essenes — must have played a part. It is especially hard to get the Essenes out of the story because there are good historical reasons for thinking that John the Baptist — the key link in the Biblical procession — was influenced by them during his Wilderness days.

asked, and I suggested that Saint Athanasius might have been wrong in founding Lavra.

"For one thing," he answered, "Saint Athanasius didn't invent monasticism. It existed already, in Egypt and the Holy Land. And there is a good reason for it, too. Ideally, the members of Christendom need unity. Christ prayed that all believers might be one. The cenobitic monastery, with its life in common, exemplifies such unity, which would be justification enough for it. But there is another reason for monasteries as well — even though, as you say, the hermit's life is on a higher level. That life is hard. It takes great strength to live it — spiritual, mental, and physical strength. So monasteries are needed as training grounds, and proving grounds, for it."

He added that, ideally, a stream of monks should be flowing to hermitages from the cenobitic monasteries, and he confessed that he himself had long wished to be a hermit, but had given the idea up recently after an experience he had had. He had set out to reconnoiter Athonite hermitages, he said, going first to spend the night at a certain *skete* that was close to some of them. He had prayed arduously that evening, for guidance, and then in the night he had had a severe attack of ulcers (from which he suffers), and had also found his positive conviction — that he wished to leave the monastery — changed. He had taken these things as signs that he should stay at Dionysiou, and he now expected to end his days there.

The Father had been talking only of cenobitic monasteries, so I asked him about the idiorrhythmic ones, and he seemed to have a low opinion of them. He said the system brought an inequality of living standards into monasteries, which was most un-Christian, and also that strict discipline, which the cenobitic abbots imposed, was vital to most monks' spiritual progress. He didn't imply that the idiorrhythmic monasteries had no good monks in them, but he seemed to think that the good ones were there in spite of the system, not because of it. And I believe his views on this point, as on others, reflected the enlightened opinion of Athos — I think he spoke with the authentic voice of the Athonite leadership.

Easter had been approaching all this time. The monks at Dionysiou, and all over Athos, had been celebrating Christ's Death, in preparation for His Resurrection. They had been reading and singing texts about these events, and going through sympathetic actions. On Good Friday, the day of the Crucifixion, they hadn't eaten a thing (if they kept the fast) till evening. Then when evening had come they had celebrated the Descent from the Cross and the Entombment.

At Dionysiou we had seen them doing this. They had used a tapestry to symbolize Christ's person. They had carried it round the church three times, in a candlelight procession; then they had carried it out to the courtyard, which is small at Dionysiou, and they had sung there. They had sung Greek sacred music, and I had heard *"Kyrie eleison"* over and over again. Then they had gone back to the church, and had held services on toward morning, but I had withdrawn and had gone to bed.

On the next day — Saturday — Christ was in the tomb, symbolically speaking. I went out walking then, and we also both spent time around the monastery. There were other guests there, too, including several Greek students and two Germans. It was hard to see things at the monastery, for the monks had scant free time to show them — if they weren't in church, or busy with chores, they were sleeping. Dionysiou is not a great sightseeing monastery, anyway. It has fine murals, in both refectory and *catholicon,* and many other treasures, but it isn't big; its court has room for the *catholicon* alone. It is picturesquely sited — high above the sea — but when we were there, at least, its windows were so dirty that they dulled the view.*

Late Saturday it began to rain a little, splattering in the courtyard. In the evening we had a frugal Lenten meal in the refectory, among the murals. Then we slept awhile, then rose before midnight, when the Resurrection was to be celebrated. This is a big thing in the Orthodox Church, where Easter outranks Christmas by far. The key symbol of the Resurrection, with the Orthodox, is the bringing of light — by a lighted candle — from the altar, and the dissemination of it through the congregation by the lighting of other candles. This the abbot, gaily vested, now began in the *catholicon.* He brought the candle from the altar, then others were lit from it, then others, and soon the whole church was ablaze. Meanwhile there was singing, and I could make out *"Kyrie eleison,"* then *"Christos anesti"* — "Christ is risen."

Then with our candles we marched out of the church, and there was more singing — *"Christos anesti"* and the rest — in the rainy courtyard. There were murals in the porches there, and their red and gold picked up the candlelight. Bells were ringing — large and small — above us, too. The singing kept on, then we went back into the church; and now all the chandeliers there — of polished

* This statement is a compliment, if anything, for on Athos cleanliness is *not* put next to Godliness. Rather it is deemed a vanity — a sign of care for superficialities — and dirtiness in a hermit, say, is well respected. Dionysiou's morale being good, the place lacked the pleasure-garden qualities of certain other monasteries.

brass, they were, with flaming candles in them — had been set to swinging to and fro. The place was full of light and movement, and it said *"Christos anesti"* — "Christ is risen" — vividly.

I went back to bed then, but the monks kept at their services till daytime. Then at seven I rose and joined them in the church once more. They were singing the liturgy — telling of the Resurrection — but soon it ended, and we all went to the refectory — laymen and monks together — to break the fast. There was fish to eat there now, and cheese, and soup, and wine. Also red-dyed hard-boiled eggs. The Greeks break these eggs against each other, saying *"Christos anesti";* and Easter eggs really mean something when treated thus — one thinks immediately of life breaking out from the tomb.

So we broke them and we feasted, meanwhile looking at the murals and listening to Father Hilarion, in the pulpit, reading. Then in time we finished, and all the strangers — the monastery's guests — went for more refreshments with the abbot. After that John Yiannias and I took our bags and stepped out in the rain. We walked steeply down to the monastery's jetty, where a caïque was waiting; and we boarded it and headed for the *cosmos.*